Indian Adolescents in the Modernising World

By the same author

—The Development of Personality in the Indian Ecology

—The Power of Politics in Governance of the Poor in India

About the Author

Dr. Margaret Khalakdina is an expert and independent consultant in the field of Human Development. She completed her Masters and Doctorate at Syracuse and Cornell Universities respectively. She has been: *Executive Director, Indian Council for Child Welfare; Dean, College of Home Science, Haryana Agricultural University, Hissar, Adviser to Vice Chancellor, Himachal Pradesh Agricultural University, Palampur.* She has also taught at Nirmala Niketan College, Mumbai and SNDT College of Home Science, Mumbai.

She has also been a Consultant to WHO and FAO in Egypt and Uganda and has also worked for UNICEF in African countries of Ethiopia and Somalia.

Dr. Khalakdina has authored and published a number of books on Early Child Care and Human Development in India, such as *Early Child Care in India (1997); Human Development in the Indian Context: A Socio-cultural Focus (two volumes, 2009 and 2011); the Development of Personality in the Indian Ecology* (2012), and *The Power of Politics in the Governance of the Poor in India* (2013). She has also contributed several articles and papers for various publications and journals on early childcare, human development and human ecology, besides contributing to seminars and discussions on topics relating to human development.

Indian Adolescents in the Modernising World

Margaret Khalakdina

CONCEPT PUBLISHING COMPANY PVT. LTD.
NEW DELHI-110059

ISBN-13 : 978-93-5125-094-4 (HB)

First Published 2015

Published and Printed by

Concept Since 1974

Concept Publishing Company Pvt. Ltd.
A/15-16, Commercial Block, Mohan Garden
New Delhi-110059 (India)
T: 25351460, 25351794, *F*: 091-11-25357109
E: publishing@conceptpub.com, W: www.conceptpub.com
Editorial Office: H-13, Bali Nagar, New Delhi-110 015, India.

Cataloging in Publication Data—*Courtesy:* D.K. Agencies (P) Ltd. <docinfo@dkagencies.com>

Khalakdina, Margaret.
Indian adolescents in the modernising world / Margaret Khalakdina.
p. cm.
Includes bibliographical references and index.
ISBN 9789351250944 (HB)
ISBN 9789351251361 (PB)

1. Teenagers—India—Social conditions. 2. Teenagers—Education—India.
3. Teenagers—India—Psychology. I. Title.

DDC 305.2350954 23

This Book is
Dedicated to
My Late Husband
Nazeem M. Khalakdina
and our Grandchildren
Isabella and Alessia Montecalvo
and
Sami and Ryan Khalakdina

Foreword

Adolescence is a period of transition from childhood to adulthood, a stage of rapid physical growth spurt and maturation. Physical and physiological developments are manifested in psycho-social behavioural and cognitive changes. During this phase, young people extend relations beyond parents and family and are influenced by peers and the world around them. The biological changes are universal, whereas the socialization process plays an important differential role in giving meaning to these changes and how these are dealt within a cultural system.

The present book, *Adolescent in India in a Modernising World*, is a timely initiative by the author towards furthering and understanding the knowledge around adolescents in India. Development during adolescence needs to be understood in its social historicity context the context of historical, sociocultural and global developments, appreciating the varied impact these factors have on the growing adolescents. In line with that approach, the present book has made an attempt to capture the transformation that is taking place in the sphere of socio-economic-geo political, educational, technological, occupational, cultural and ideological aspects influencing youth development in India as a result of global changes in the last few decades. The uneven distribution of the positive results of development are highlighted, emphasizing how a large number of adolescents have remained untouched by new opportunities for advancement that are currently available in the modernizing world of affluence in India.It also tries to offer some probable solutions to overcome, threats and risks faced by the majority of growing adolescents and to harness their competencies as per the parameters of the Millennium Goals.

Adolescents currently comprise a large segment of our population, numbering 243 million. Interestingly, of the world's total adolescents comprising 1.25 billion, India is the home to every fifth of the youngsters in the age group of 10-19 years. We are witnessing currently the largest ever generation of adolescents in India; it is a unique opportune moment to capitalize on the *open demographic window* by shaping their capabilities as human resource that holds the nation's future. Appropriate timely investments in meeting their holistic developmental needs in the areas of health, nutrition, education and promoting occupational competence is imperative for mobilizing their potential and launch a socio-economic transformation. It is perhaps the best strategy to break the cycle of poverty and inequality so prevalent in our country. We may lose out on the potential of a generation by limited investment and inadequate provisions that is likely to not only deprive youth from growing optimally but also may result in their and the nation facing serious consequences in the development of the young.

It is heartening, that the author has effectively delved on the above conceptual framework and presented it across the chapters of the book. It offers perspectives of allied disciplines of social science, skilfully interwoven in presenting the comprehensive approach to understand the profile of the adolescent set within the Indian context. It has added valuable insights about the development, behaviour and personality characteristics Indian youth emerging from the heterogeneity and homogeneity of the ecology that surrounds them. There is a judicious mix of empirical evidence, theoretical and philosophical information in the text of the volume.

I recall in 2004 when I was drafting the document *Adolescents in India—A Profile for the UN System*, the non-availability of relevant data and empirical evidence on young people was felt as a major constraint in portraying the profile of the Indian youth and for supporting and corroborating evidence based advocacy as also the strategies required for intervention. However, I am pleased to note that the book has cited several pieces of indigenous research available on issues and dealt with the challenge of paucity of information relating to adolescents growing in heterogeneous cultures within India. The relationship between the developing adolescent, process of socialization, ecology and values related to Indian culture has been interlinked in a convincing manner. As you read through the chapters from beginning to the end focusing on the cumulative determinants that make up adolescent's identity and challenges confronted by them in the process reflect adequately and appropriately to the Indian context.

I feel honoured, to be given an opportunity by the author, Dr. Margaret Khalakdina, to introduce her book to a wide range of readers comprising academia, policy-makers, parents, voluntary organizations, civil society and development partners and all others concerned with development of adolescents. We know that as the emerging generation stands on the threshold of adulthood, they need to be nurtured and provided support to grow optimally. We all have a collective responsibility to ensure that this stage of human life becomes an age of opportunity having an enabling supportive environment. The illustrious author of the book has provided us with information which is comprehensive to understand the milieu in which the adolescents grow and develop. It is hoped that this enhanced conceptual understanding will facilitate, formulation of supportive policies, designing of effective interventions, using of effective strategies for capacity building, advocacy, and creating synergy within and across institutions to make Indian youth flourish and transform the nation in to a vibrant society.

Adarsh Sharma
Former Director,
National Institute of Public Cooperation
and Child Development (NIPCCD),
and
Team Leader
IDA funded Technical Assistant Agency-ICDS
Systems Strengthening and Nutrition
Improvement Project (ISSNIP)

Acknowledgements

I acknowledge the sincerity, dedication and hard work of Mr. M.K. Shaji and Mrs. Shakuntala Dixit without whose assistance and cooperation this book would have been difficult to complete. I thank them most sincerely.

I also wish to express my sincere gratitude to my children Rolando, Asheena, Arshad and Madga who have encouraged me in this endeavour.

I am also grateful to several of my friends and colleagues who have given me their valuable advice.

M. Khalakdina

Contents

Contents

Introduction

The present globalised world reflects many changes from the past in different spheres—socio-economic, geo-political, educational, technological, occupational, demographic, cultural and ideological. From the early 1990s, when the Government of India decidedly embarked upon the policies of Liberalisation, Privatisation and Globalisation, the socio-economic life of the Indians, firmly linked as it is to the happenings in the globalised world, has inexorably been undergoing a process of transformation. New levels and dimensions of riches and comforts have been created by the technological innovations and increased production of goods and services, and trade and business. In this context of the inevitable transformation, the parameters of human development and well-being are clearly different from the days gone by. However, the riches and comforts resulted from new technological innovations and communication facilities of the modern world are unevenly distributed. In India, as also in other countries of the under-developed world, there are large numbers of people who remain not significantly affected by the positive developments of the modern globalised world. The Millennium Goals formulated in 2000 has drawn up a road-map of development for the world population who lag behind in various parameters of development and welfare. The Millennium Goals aims to:

- Eradicate extreme poverty and hunger;
- Achieving universal primary education;
- Promoting gender equality and empowering women;

- Reducing Child Mortality;
- Improving Maternal Health;
- Combating HIV/AIDS, Malaria and other epidemic diseases;
- Ensuring Environmental Sustainability; and
- Developing a Global Partnership for Development (*United Nations website: http://www.un.org/millennium goals/ bkgd.shtml. Retrieved on 01 August, 2012*).

The present book while discussing the current status of Indian adolescents in terms of the important parameters stated in the Millennium Development Goals. It also tries to offer some probable solutions to overcome the impediments faced by the country, dwells on different socio-psychological aspects of adolescent development in India in the context of the changed parameters of well-being, new opportunities for advancement, and social and cultural changes that have taken place in the modernizing world of developing India.

In the first chapter, a general picture of the adolescent segment of Indian people is given covering the demographic, educational, health, nutritional and occupational aspects.

The second chapter presents theoretical knowledge on adolescent development in India. Presently, there is much information on socio-psychological aspects of adolescent development in general, but there is very few and scattered research on these aspects relating to adolescent development in specific heterogeneous cultures within India. The third chapter deals with the psyche of Indian adolescents. This chapter deals with the adolescents among upper and middle classes, especially affected by the many challenges they face in achieving competence for availing of opportunities for success in life and also the adolescents belonging to the lower socio-economic classes affected by the despairing situations of their inability to get a completed education, joblessness and frustration at having to live in the midst of apparent affluence and riches flaunted by the richer adolescents.

The fourth chapter entitled "The Influence of the Family and the Relational Network" analyse the strength of the influence of parents and other relations on adolescents in the changing world, where the children get more accustomed to newer values and ideologies which are quite different from those of their parents. During the socialisation process the parents tend to reinforce their adolescents according to their own goal aspirations, whereas the children attempt to develop their own goals. In this process of interaction, there are often confrontations, especially in family situations caused by divorce, single-parenthood, and both parents having to work hard outside home leaving little time left to pay attention to the behaviour of adolescents. Adolescents in such situations tend to express behaviour that is deviant from the familial and socio-cultural norms. The chapter also discusses influence of teachers, the peer groups and the neighbourhood on the psychological development of the adolescent. The limitations that surround the adolescents during this chronological stage of development have also been discussed. The chapter also discusses many other types of influences on adolescents within the human and social networks and how the individual psyche of the individual adolescent plays a great role in meeting with the demands of others.

The fifth chapter entitled "Communication of Values between Generations" discusses the various issues arising from the old and new generations of parents and children respectively. The chapter also discusses changes in the mode of communication between the parental generation and the adolescent generation. How the process of value transference from the old generation to the new generation occurs in the dynamism of change has been discussed. Also discussed is the pivotal role that social media plays in the thinking and behaviour of adolescents.

The sixth chapter deals with Heterosexual Relations in Adolescence, which form an important sphere of interaction between the sexes as they develop socio-psychological features of attraction towards the opposite sex.

The seventh chapter is on how the adolescent deals with other than the family network and discusses the next most important network of influence, namely the peer group. The context of interaction with the peer group scales several different types of peers during adolescence: those in the immediate neighbourhood, those in the wider context of the schooling system and those with whom the adolescent interacts with at macro level as the adolescent develops wider contextual relations.

The eighth chapter deals with educational attainments and the various ways in which the adolescent learns about the world around him and gains the necessary professional attributes to contend with new knowledge and technology as they impinge upon the adolescents.

Each generation faces a new world structure and new systems of interaction. The adolescents of today, unlike those of the previous decades, are faced with a new world characterised by increased inter-linkages between and among different countries. This is propelled by the world of social media and the use of computers and other gadgets of communication. This new world of great technological advances widens the gap between the old and the new generation. The new generation is faced with the loosening ties with the traditional world of the past decades and with their parenting generation. India is a heterogeneous amalgam of differing sub-cultures, which are mainly rural. The effects of the exposure to the technologically advanced global world are differentially experienced by the adolescents in the rural and urban areas. Therefore, within the world of adolescents, there is also likely to be a clash between the rural and urban.

Homogeneity is ensconced in religion, but heterogeneity is diverse as reflected in socio-economic, demographic and related spheres. Inspite of the various definitions of modernity, there are certain core values in every society and, therefore, the clash between the old and the new will continue. It, therefore, becomes a challenge for the adolescents to face modernising changes in a futuristic manner.

The last chapter focuses on the various cumulative factors that shape the world of the adolescents in self identity. The adolescent vacilates between finding an equilibrium status between himself and the changing world around him. He grows from being an emerging crysillus to a full grown self perceived systematic entity. Some events have a forceful impact on his personality while others are barely glancing influences. Nevertheless, they combine to make a unique image both introspectively and extrospectively.

1

The Meaning of Adolescence, the Range of Demographic and Educational Features

The term adolescence is said to be a derivative from the Latin word *adolescere*, which means to grow up or to grow into maturity (*Muuss, R.E., 1990*; *Bronfenbrenner, 1989*). There are varying academic perspectives in defining and characterising the period of adolescence. The Biological definition of adolescence emphasises the physical and sexual changes occurring in an individual beginning with puberty. These changes indicate the development of the individual towards physical and mental maturity. Psychologically, an adolescent is characterized in terms of the chronological developmental tasks to be accomplished, the central task to be accomplished by an adolescent being to achieve a personal identity. Sociologically, adolescents are defined in terms of their status within society, specifically, as a transitional period between childhood and adulthood. During this period, the adolescent is assumed to begin to take responsibility for his actions within his familial and societal framework.

The nature of role-behaviour is one of the indicators of psychological maturity of an adolescent. Expected psychological maturity during adolescence and the corresponding social status accorded to adolescents differ from culture to culture.

The development of maturity begins from early childhood, growing in complexity through the primary school years to the stage of the adolescence. Through the course of maturity development, the individual acquires various skills related to growing independent, decision-making and responsibility for action.

According to G. Stanley Hall, whose two-volume work on the period of adolescence is considered to be the first scientific study in this field, adolescence is a period of "stress and storm" (*Hall, 1904*).

Adolescence is a two-sided coin in its description as to who this individual is and how can one recognize this individual as an adolescent. The behaviourists find a fitting description in terms of the type of maturity, self-control and independence that the adolescent displays. Other psychologists have their own markers like Erickson's stage of identity *vs.* confusion (*Erickson, E., 1950*) and Freud's phallic and genital stages in psycho-sexual development (*Freud, S., 1953*).

It is assumed by the chronologist that by the time the individual reaches his teens, he is no longer a child, but is moving towards young adulthood. Adolescence is a combination of maturity and immaturity exhibited at different times under different circumstances. An adolescent's behaviour is mainly inferred to be mature when he is able to think and act in a manner that is not child-like but take responsibility for his behaviour. There is a great amount of vacillation in behaviour during adolescence.

A marker of adolescent development is pubertal changes. These pubertal changes, however, need not necessarily imply the occurrence of mature behaviour. The concept of maturity is a mixed package of self-control and self-motivation (*Maslow, Abraham, 1943*). Allport describes maturity as when an individual exhibits moral and spiritual values in his behaviour. Productive orientation is yet another description of an individual's maturity in his behaviour (*Allport, 1955*). In Carl Roger's description of the attainment of maturity, as an individual moves towards adolescence he exhibits a mature behaviour which reflects an understanding of others (*Rogers, 1961*). According to Eric Erickson, an individual attains maturity when he is able to resolve his identity crisis and has knowledge of who he is (*Erickson, 1868*). Adler identifies adolescence as the period when the individual overcomes a sense of inferiority and develops a sense of self-confidence (*Adler, Alfred, 1935*). Achieving a sense of equilibrium between one's own self and the demands of others is said to be the stage when one exhibits mature behaviour. Thus, a variety of qualitative definitions seem to make up a holistic description of a maturing individual moving through the period of adolescence. The major theme, however, is self-control, responsibility, logical decision-making powers and the ability to arrive at compromises between oneself and the society around, yet upholding one's individuality.

The study of adolescence as a behavioural/cultural concept overcomes the inadequacies in the traditional attempts to define the term adolescence chronologically, physically or legally (*B. Geralden Lambert, et al.*). In the chronological definition, adolescence is tied to an age-span, with the starting age generally varying from 10 to 13 and the concluding age varying from 19 to 21, depending on which definition is prevalent. Many researchers and developmental specialists in the U.S. use the age span 10-24 years as a working definition of adolescence (*Office of Population Affairs, 2013*). However, there is general agreement in India that an adolescent is one who has attained emotional and physiological maturity and is at the foothills of moving upwards towards young adulthood, and chronologically the adolescence is taken to be from the age of 13 to 18. The latter is incidentally considered the legal age in India. At this age, the adolescent is expected to display a sense of independence indicative of responsible decision-making and self-control. The importance of family and training in life-skills in the adolescent years is especially important for those who have not had adequate education and are uninformed about the world around them.

In the Indian context, the expected role-behaviour of adolescents varies in differing ecological areas. In rural ecologies, for instance, responsibility-taking often occurs early, almost during the primary school years, when the child is expected to help in occupational and household chores, take care of younger siblings and, in several instances, to be responsible for the whole range of familial tasks in accordance with the customary norms and practices of the society. Work in rural areas mainly relates to cultivation and other petty manual works related to farming like that involved in small smithery and petty crafts needed for the village agricultural community.

In urban areas, adolescence is tied to educational markers like senior school, high school and such like titles given to the group entering this stage of educational attainment. Therefore, adolescence in urban areas tends to be standardized with school education.

In tribal areas, adolescence is formally acknowledged by rites of passage for the male child or the attainment of menarchy by the female child (*Van Gennep, A., 1960*). The latter is a social message spread out through the community that the particular family whose female child has attained puberty is now ready for her marriage, and marriage negotiators are kept busy finding a match for the girl from the same or nearby villages. Caste and ethnicity are significant requirements for marriage. In many traditional families in India, symbolic marriage is conducted between the female and male even before the girl attains puberty. After the attainment of puberty, which may be anywhere between earlier period of adolescence (12 to 13 years) and the later period, the ceremony of *gauna* is conducted and the consummation of marriage and the real conjugal life begins after this *gauna* ceremony.

Demographic Profile of Adolescents in India

India is said to have the largest national population of adolescents. According to the data from the 2011 Census of

India, about 19.19 per cent of the population in India are adolescents, who are between the ages of 10 to 19 (*Census of India, 2011*). There are 232.3 million persons in this age-group; 122.5 millions of them are male and 109.8 millions are female.

As India like the rest of the world is rapidly becoming urbanized, more adolescents tend to move towards urban areas (*UNICEF, 2012*) and they mostly concentrate in congested areas. The proportion of the Indian population living in urban areas increased from 27.81 per cent in 2001 to 31.16 per cent in 2011 (*Registrar General and Census Commissioner, 2011*). The socio-economic conditions in which the majority of these adolescents live can be inferred from the household survey data of the Census of India, 2011. These data show, among other things that—

- 27.5 per cent of the urban households live in rented houses.
- Only 52.9 per cent of the urban households live in concrete houses, the rest are just liveable houses or dilapidated houses.
- Only 47.4 per cent of the urban households have cemented floor.
- 13 per cent of the urban households do not have washrooms.
- 18.6 per cent of the urban households do not have toilets.

Millions of adolescents in India do not enjoy access to general, sexual and reproductive healthcare, quality education and opportunities for skill development. This is in spite of the fact that the importance of equal access to early child-care, education, nutrition, health and provision of a protective environment to every child has been acknowledged by the various policy and planning documents in India in its various documents (see, for example, the Report of the Working Group on Child Rights for the Twelfth Five Year Plan, 2012-2017).

Health and Nutrition

A total of 56 per cent of females and 30 per cent of males in this age group are anaemic, which is the sixth highest rate in the world. This places the country along with the least developed African nations (*UNICEF, 2012*). Anaemia increases the maternal risk of haemorrhage and sepsis during childbirth, as well as increasing cognitive and physical problems in young children. At the same time, it reduces productivity in adults.

Nearly half of the Indian female children aged 15 to 19 are underweight. "Such under-nutrition renders adolescents vulnerable to disease and early death, and has lifelong health consequences," says the report. "In adolescent mothers, under nutrition is related to slow foetal growth and low birth-weight."

The mortality rate is comparatively less among adolescents which indicates that they are biologically stronger at this chronological age.

Table 1.1: Age-Specific Mortality Rates

Age Group	1980		1990		1995		1998		1991	
	F	M	F	M	F	M	F	M	F	M
0-4	43.5	40.1	27.9	24.8	25.3	23.2	24.1	21.0	21.1	19.8
5-9	4.0	3.0	2.8	2.3	2.7	2.2	2.4	2.1	2.1	1.6
10-14	1.7	1.7	1.4	1.4	1.4	1.3	1.2	1.0	1.3	1.2
15-19	2.9	2.0	2.5	1.7	2.0	1.7	2.0	1.7	2.1	1.7
20-24	3.8	2.3	3.1	2.4	2.7	2.1	2.7	2.3	2.8	2.3
35-39	4.6	4.4	3.2	3.9	3.1	3.7	3.0	4.2	2.8	4.8
45-49	7.3	9.6	6.3	9.0	5.2	8.1	5.2	7.4	5.3	8.5
55-59	16.7	21.5	14.4	20.9	11.8	17.5	13.7	18.9	13.0	19.4
All ages	12.4	12.4	9.6	9.7	8.7	9.3	8.8	9.2	8.2	8.9

Source: *Central Statistical Organization, 1999: Women and Men in India* 1998, page 10.

Table 1.1 indicates that the female adolescents have a higher mortality rate than the males due to their vulnerability and poor care given by the family due to social norms, where in contrast to the male, the girl child is a discounted child. In

1999, mortality in the age group 10-14 was 1.2 for males and 1.3 for females and for the age group 15-19, the mortality was 1.7 for males and 2.0 for females. For the child-bearing age-group of 20-24 years, the mortality rate is higher. Almost 47 per cent of females in the age group of 11 to 19 years are underweight in India, which is the highest rate in the world (*UNICEF, 2012*). Female mortality rates are higher as compared to male mortality rates across all ages. It is particularly noticeable for the child-bearing age group (20-24 years) and indicating a dip over the years which could be due to increased access to healthcare facilities in the highly populated States of India like UP, West Bengal, Tamil Nadu, Andhra Pradesh, Maharashtra, Bihar which have larger proportion of adolescents.

A study of prevalence of overweight and obesity in Indian adolescents found that, age-adjusted overweight was prevalent among 14.3 per cent of males and 9.2 per cent of females while the prevalence of obesity was 2.9 per cent in males and 1.5 per cent in females. The prevalence of overweight among children was higher in middle socio-economic classes as compared to high socio-economic classes in both males and females. Eating habits like junk food, chocolate, eating outside at weekend and physical inactivity like lack of exercise and sports have contributed to overweight *(Goyal, et al., 2010)*.

Age at Marriage

In India a large number of people get married before entering adulthood, i.e., at the stage of adolescence, although the mean age at marriage has been increasing steadily from 1951 onwards both for males and females. The mean age at marriage is at present 19.6 years for females and 24.5 years for males. This indicates that females marry earlier than males (*UNFPA, 2003*). The Table 1.2 indicates the mean age at marriage for males and females.

Table 1.2: Mean Age at Marriage in India

Year	*Female*	*Male*
1951	15.4	19.9
1961	16.1	22.3
1971	17.1	22.7
1981	17.9	23.3
1992	19.5	NA
1996	19.4	NA
1997	19.5	NA
1998	19.5	NA
1999	19.6	NA

In 1998-99, sixty one per cent of women in the age group of 20-24 years were married before the age of 18 years. Out of these 59 per cent were from the rural areas and 41 per cent were from the urban areas (*NFHS, 1999*). The number of females who were married before the age of 18 years has decreased from 54 per cent in 1992-93 to 43 per cent in 2007-08 (*UNICEF, 2012*). But still the figure is the eighth highest in the world and Pakistan fares much better with just 25 per cent of females being married before the age of 18 years.

In general terms, it is obvious that the health and nutritional statuses of Indian adolescents are indices of their poor well-being, especially of the female adolescents.

Education

Education for the primary-school-aged children has for long been a constitutionally-mandated priority in India. However, its implementation is far from satisfactory. According to 2001 Census of India, 19.37 per cent of adolescents in India were found to be illiterate and 21.15 per cent, though literate, did not complete primary school education, making a total of 40.52 per cent of adolescents who have not had primary school education.

Table 1.3: Selected demographic and reproductive health variables among women of the child-bearing age

Region (and States)	*Among women 15–49*					*Among women 20–24, % who marry before*	
	Total fertility rate (lifetime births per woman)	*% with ≥ 6 yrs. Education*	*% living in rural areas*	*% using a modern method**	*% of women whose most recent birth was attended by a professional*	*Age 18*	*Age 20*
North (Delhi, Haryana, Himachal Pradesh, Jammu & Kashmir, Punjab, Rajasthan and Uttarakhand)	2.64	53.0	63.0	54.9	54.0	26.8	44.9
Central (Chhattisgarh, Madhya Pradesh and Uttar Pradesh)	3.53	33.5	73.9	39.5	32.9	52.9	72.5
East (Bihar, Jharkhand, Orissa and West Bengal)	2.99	36.9	76.3	40.9	37.2	51.8	70.1
North East (Arunachal Pradesh, Assam, Manipur, Meghalaya, Mizoram, Nagaland, Sikkim and Tripura)	2.61	57.3	71.5	32.1	43.2	26.6	41.9
West (Goa, Gujarat and Maharashtra)	2.21	63.5	49.8	57.7	74.2	32.4	50.9
South (Andhra Pradesh, Karnataka, Kerala and Tamil Nadu)	1.88	54.9	60.3	62.7	81.2	37.1	54.0

Source: Moore, A. M. et al., Adolescent Marriage and child bearing in India : Current situation and recent trends, New York: Guttmacher Institute, 2009.

Very few are able to complete high school education. Fewer go to college. Therefore, coupled with poor indices of health and yet poorer indices of educational attainment, it is obvious that the average adolescent is less geared towards well-being and attainment of professional skills. Part of the problem is that there is little parental reinforcement, and part of it is that the infrastructure and trained personnel are inadequate. These factors do not encourage the adolescent, especially the female, to attain a state of well-being. The result is obvious. Less robustness of males and lesser than the standard requirement of female health are major factors which destabilize acceptable standards of well-being among adolescents in India.

The social reality of the situation is that most of these adolescents with poor health and educational statuses are to be found in the poverty stricken sections of the society, especially in rural and tribal areas.

These are, however, not the only factors that intervene in depleting the potentials of cognition and creative development in these disadvantaged groups which make up about 70 per cent of the total population of the country. This proportion of the adolescent population is barriered by lack of facilities. Turning to the economic factor, we find that most of these youngsters have by force to work at meagre paying jobs such as casual labour, manual work in family occupations, shop assistants and such like, in order to earn a survival living standard (*Sharma, 2006*). A recent study conducted in 25 districts of Tamil Nadu State has reported that 87 per cent adolescents in the age-group of 14-18 work in the unorganized sector ("87 per cent adolescents work as an unorganized workforce", Express News Service, Chennai, 3 October, 2013).

According to the data from Census 2001, there were 12.7 million economically active children in the age-group of 5-14 years. 2.3 per cent of all the children in the age group of 5-14 years were workers. There were 87 million children (5-14) who were out of school during 2001.

These young adolescents become little factories of unskilled production doing lowly jobs which, according to psychologists, bring about prolonged deprivation of mental and cognitive skills, depriving them of the inherent potential that exists in each one of them (*Misra, 2002*).

Prolonged deprivation has obvious consequences. It leads to the loss of cognitive functions and the ability of individuals to be proactive and progressive (*Saraswathi, 2003*). It also brings about apathy, lack of incentives and dependency upon the environment without becoming proactive.

However, these are not the only factors that affect the individual's capacity. There are several strands of subtle influences that emanate from the environment. Cultural and ecological factors, for instance, play a significant role on the development of the growing individual. This is more important in the stage of adolescent growth, where the adolescent begins to develop his own personality and identity. He is more especially sensitively susceptible to changes in cultural and ecological factors. Chief amongst the cultural factors are the processes of socialisation and the effect of parenting influences on the identity of the adolescent (*Sapre Saloni, 2006*). The lack of appropriate parenting and basic essentials for survival also affect adolescent development (*Khalakdina, M., 1979*).

The everyday activities of the family inculcate into a developing personality, from the early years of childhood, through adolescence and into adulthood the learning of the occupational skills (*Havighurst, R. J., 1972*). Such skills change from one ecology to another, i.e. rural, urban; plains, mountainous, desert, sea coast. The adolescents growing up in rural agricultural families tend to be attuned to skills which are necessary for agricultural and related occupational tasks. In urban ecologies, available choices of occupations are manifold, but skills to enter into different urban occupations, which can provide better livelihoods, than in rural areas need to be learned and practiced largely from non-family sources. Those who can afford better education can make best of the opportunities in urban ecologies and be upwardly mobile. Thus, the adolescent is more geo-ecologically bound in rural and tribal areas, whereas in the urban areas the adolescent can move occupationally in vertical manner. The farmer's son continues to be a farmer or if he is more proactive than doing just that, he might move to an urban area in search of desultory jobs where no skills or only manual skills are required. This is obvious when we view public spaces like railway stations, market places, bus-stops, where youngsters gather around as porters earning what they can for the day, but nothing substantial or consistent.

Geo-ecological factors have a subtle effect on the behaviour of the youngsters as they grow. A fisherman's child tends to remain a fisherman. A shepherd's son in the upper ranges of the Himalayas tends to remain sheep-keeper, and in cities that are crowded like in Mumbai and Delhi children from primary school age continue to throng market places, where desultory jobs are required like carrying and fetching for tradesmen. They also tend to work the service jobs as at the barber shop, as helper in a super market, but all lowly and hardly stimulating for increasing cognitive development (*Weiner, 1991*). Those adolescents who are sharp and clever turn to devious ways such as stealing and selling pots (drugs) or indulging in non-socially approved behaviour.

Given all these influencing variables, it is difficult to identify which of them have priority in having significant effects on the development of the adolescent, especially in the poorer sections of the population. For example, delinquents will continue be delinquents till they are caught and put into a juvenile home. This does not mean that they are reformed. When let out, on the assumption that they are cured, they may go back to their original habits as do alcoholic individuals (*Clayton A. Hartjen, 1982*).

Socialisation into social norms is a major foundation of imparting societal values to the young. However, if the equilibrium in the home situation is not reinforcing, children tend to go astray.

Let us take an example: Living in a large metropolis is a cluster of poor ethnic groups. Females are married off early and bear children in quick succession, the father unable to earn enough to sustain the family, becomes frustrated in his poor paying job since he is not as well educated as he should be to get a higher paying job. Neither is the rest of his family. The father tends to turn to gambling and drinking. Berated by his wife and the demands of his children, he indulges in domestic abuse. He sobers down after a while, goes back to his job, or if dismissed, because of his untimely appearances at work, he looks for another work and another with short periods of work as he earns no money for his own anti-social habits. The vicious cycle goes on. These families do not know the meaning of divorce or the wife is unable to pay for the divorce proceedings and then in any case she is socially stigmatized if she leaves her husband (*Choudhary, J.N., 1988*). So in despair the cycle continues forcing the young children who are growing up watching such misery, they themselves take to bad habits like smoking drugs, inhaling anti-stabilising products, eating tobacco and stealing in order to get money to continue in their bad habits. This is not unusual as social learning theory tells us that children tend to imitate the behaviour of their parents (*Bandura, A., 1977*).

This is not the story of one family, but of several living in *jhuggi-jhonpri* squalor.

Thus, we see that there are two major factors that indicate the parameters of adolescence, namely chronological age and educational attainment. Besides these, as given in the following chapters, are characteristics in the social and economic environments that also influence the makings of an adolescent as an identity. In this chapter, we have mainly indicated the larger scenario of age and age-related educational attainment. The real makings of adolescence are from other environmental influences like the family, the peer group, and, more especially, the inner inherent self-analysis (*Kakar and Chowdhury, 1970*) that causes the adolescent to build his own identity.

REFERENCES

Adler, Alfred, 1935, "The Fundamental view of individual psychology", *International Journal of Indian Psychology*. 1, pp. 5-8.

Allport, G.W., 1955, *Becoming*. New Haven: Yale University Press.

Bandura, A., 1977, *Social Learning Theory*. Englewood Cliffs, New Jersey: Prentice Hall.

Bronfenbrenner, 1989, "Ecological Systems Theory", *Annals of Child Development*, 6: 185-246.

Census of India, 2011. Table C-3. *Single Year Age Returns by Residence and Sex*.

Choudhary, J.N., 1988, *Divorce in Indian Society*, Jaipur: Rupa Books.

Clayton A. Hartjen, 1982, "Delinquency, Development, and Social Integration in India", *Social Problems*, Vol. 29, No. 5 (June 1982), pp. 464-473.

Erickson, E.H., 1950, *Childhood and Society*. New York: Norton.

Erickson, E.H., 1968, Identity: *Youth and Crisis*. New York: Norton.

Freud, S., 1953, '*Three Essays on Sexuality*', in J. Strachey (ed.), *The Standard Edition of the Complete Psychological Works of Sigmund Freud*, Volume VII, pp. 135-243. London: Hogarth.

Geralden, Lambert B.; Barbara, F.; Rothschild, Richard Altland; Laurence B. Green, 1978, *Adolescence: Transition from Childhood to Maturity*. Chapter 1: "What is Adolescence", p. 1. California: Rooks & Cole Publishing Company.

Goyal, R.K.; Shah, V.N.; Saboo, B.D.; Phatak, S.R.; Shah, N.N.; Goel, M.C.; Raval, P.B.; and Patel, S.S., 2010, "Prevalence of overweight and obesity in Indian adolescent school-going children: Its relationship with socio-economic status and associated lifestyle factors", *Journal of Associations of Physicians India*, 58, pp. 151-58.

Hall, G. Stanley, 1904, "Adolescence: Its Psychology and its Relations to Physiology, Anthropology, Sociology, Sex, Crime, Religion, and Education". New York: Appleton-Century Crofts.

Havighurst, R.J., 1972, *Developmental Tasks and Education*. 3rd ed., New York: McKay.

Kakar, S., and K. Chowdhury, 1970, *Conflict and Choice: Indian Youth in a Changing Society*. Bombay: Somaiya.

Khalakdina, M., 1979, *Early Child Care in India*. London/New York/Paris: Gordon and Breach.

Maslow, Abraham, 1943, "A Theory of Human Motivation." *Psychological Review*, Vol. 50, No. 4, pp. 370-396.

Misra, Girishwar, 2002, "Deprivation and Cognitive Competence" in

Dalal, A.K. and Girishwar Misra, *New Directions in Indian Psychology*, Vol. 1, pp. 280-300.

Muuss, R.E., 1990, *Adolescent Behaviour and Society: A Book of Readings* (4th ed.), New York: McGraw Hill.

Office of Population Affairs, US Department of Health and Human Services, *OAPP Adolescent Brain Development,http://www.hhs.gov/opa/familylife/tech_assistance/etraining/adolescent_brain/Overview/what_is_adolescence/index.html, retrieved on 4.2.2013.*

Registrar General and Census Commissioner, India, 15th July, 2011, Rural Urban Distribution of Population (provisional population totals).

Rogers, C., 1961, *On Becoming a Person*. Cambridge, Mass: Riverside.

Report of the Working Group on Child Rights for the Twelfth Five Year Plan (2012-2017), Ministry of Women and Child Development, Government of India.

Sapre, Saloni, 2006, "Parenting and Adolescent Identity: A Study of Indian Families in New Delhi and Geneva", *Journal of Adolescent Research*, Vol. No. 5, pp. 484-513.

Saraswathi, T.S., 2003, 'Introduction', in T.S. Saraswathi (ed.), *Cross-cultural Perspective in Human Development*, pp. 23-47. New Delhi: Sage.

Sharma, Usha, 2006, *Child Labour in India*. New Delhi: Mittal Publications.

UNFPA, December 2003, *Adolescents in India*: A Profile.

UNICEF, 2012, *The State of the World's Children*, 2012.

United Nations, 2012, http://www.un.org/millenniumgoals/bkgd.shtml. Retrieved on 1 August, 2012.

Van Gennep, A., 1960, *The Rites of Passage*, Chicago. Chicago University Press.

Weiner, M., 1991, *The Child and the State in India: Child Labour and Education Policy in Comparative Perspective*. Princeton, NJ: Princeton University Press.

2

Theoretical Paradigms of Adolescent Development

It is important to start by fixing the parameters of theoretical and empirical concepts with regard to development during adolescence, which is a specific chronological time-period of physical, mental and social development of an individual. Therefore, we will set the stage by selecting theoretical conceptualizations that bring into profile this chronological period of development. The basic theoretical conceptualizations on adolescence are related to theories of behaviour that are both perceptible internally as well as observable in the behaviour, speech and attitudes of the adolescent, as being typically belonging to a particular age-range. The Stimulus-Response theory sets the foundation for an understanding of behaviour throughout the human life-span. As regards adolescent development, the theory of Watson (*Watson, J.B., 1913*) refers to the varied influences which stimulate growth processes during adolescence. Skinner (*1974*) and other behaviourist theorists like Thorndike (*Thorndike, 1905*) and Hull (*Hull, 1943*) emphasize that human behaviour relates directly to stimuli from the environment and are conditioned and reinforced positively or negatively, affecting the individual/individuals. The most popular theoretical frame is conditioned response which if applied to adolescent development states paradigmatically that:

(1) The developing human being is affected by stimuli both externally and internally—externally by interaction with the outside world and internally by stimuli which originate cognitively within the psyche of the individual (*Watson, 1913; Skinner, 1974*).

(2) These maturational experiences are like building blocks in the human being. As the individual grows through the chronological stage of adolescent development, he is imbued with growing complex interactive experiences which contribute to his cognitive maturity, psychological development and the learning of societal mores. These interactive experiences relate to the events in the external world which provide stimuli to which the growing individual acts and reacts, modifying his already existing cognitive development. It is but natural that the larger and the more experiences the adolescent accumulates the more his knowledge deepens and he assimilates the characteristics of "growing up". In the growing years, till the individual reaches his physiological growth peak at adulthood, there are two spurts of physical growth. The first spurt is in the pre-school years and the second is in the adolescent years (*Diamond et al., 2001*).

(3) These cognitive experiences expressed in behaviour are basically related to the concepts of cognitive theorists, the most popular being those of Piaget and Inhelder (*Piaget and Inhelder, 1969*).

(4) The fourth important aspect of the paradigm is that heredity and nurture interplay with each other in the development process. Heredity is conventionally recognized as a source of genetic inheritance, from the parent generation to the child generation, of characteristics. In this aspect, the human being exhibits traits related to his biological determinacy according to the epigenetic rules of the appearance of behaviour in the species (*Thomas, R. Murray, 2001*).

(5) Development is holistic. In other words, there is interplay between and among different developmental frames. It is to say that the interplay is between and among psychological, sociological and economic factors. The behaviour of the growing adolescents can be attributed to the totality of the influences of the environmental stimulating experiences. There are dynamic interchanges among these varying influencing factors.

Sometimes the psychological inner workings of the adolescent mind are predominant. Sometimes the stimuli from the family and closer community networks influence behavioural traits more than other factors. At other times, the general societal, economic and political situations play dominant roles. For example, an economic recession affects all human beings to some extent or the other, and in India the political turmoil in the Kashmir valley or the social upheavals created by the Naxalites in other parts of the country might be affecting greatly the psyche of the adolescent minds. All these varying aspects affect the canalization of the maturing of the individual to some degree or the other. Currently, a great concern is the geo-ecological and climatic changes in the environment which affect the behaviour of the human being (*Irwin Altman and Joachim Wohlwill, 1977*). However, the relevance of the climatic and geo-ecological factors has to be explored to find out such factors which relate to the development of the adolescent in different settings. For example, an adolescent growing up in the Thar desert might have different perceptions, conceptualizations and attitudes towards his environment from the one that is growing up in the upper ranges of the Himalayas. Such like differences abound which are yet to be explored and explained. We might take these examples even further. For instance, that a delinquent adolescent falls back into delinquency even after his experiences in a remand home. Why does the female adolescent continue to be subdued in spite of being domestically abused in her early marriage years. These are areas of explanation which need expansion in order that more knowledge is gained about the period of growth called adolescence.

Explanations of developmental behaviour depend upon which theoretical frame is being referred to. For example, when describing the influences of society on development, the theory of Erickson (*Erickson, 1963*) is the most favoured, especially in the description of the chronological stages of development.

Outward behaviour as perceived, analysed and explored is also inherent in the workings of the mind. In other words the psychoanalytical paradigms of Freudian psychology and neo-Freudian psychology is now in much profile especially as stimuli are increasing in complexity leading to further understanding of behaviour stimulated by the inner psyche (*Kakar, S., 1981*). The stages of psychosexual development are the well-known paradigms of psychoanalytical explanation of behaviour. This Freudian theory is of much utility in the adolescent years as it relates to the phallic and the genital years of development, for it is during these years that heterosexual development is stimulated, and the adolescent has to cope with different heterosexual needs competing for expression (*Freud, S., 1953*). With the increasing complexity in the affairs of the world, psychoanalysis, especially of the adolescent, is accruing more importance in the explanations of why the adolescent behaves the way he does, especially with regard to heterosexuality and in episodes of psychological depression, anxiety and conflict. For instance, guidance and counselling for adolescents is clearly related to psychoanalysis and its utility as the characteristic process.

Adolescent behaviour is also related to cultural and social values as defined by ethnicity, caste/community, religion and geo-ecology. Bronfenbrenner, who is well-known for his explanations about micro, meso, exo and macro ecologies, offers vivid explanations of culturally-toned behaviour.

Other micro theories that subscribe to explanations of adolescent behaviour are Atkinson's explanation of motivation and need-achievement which assumes a high profile in the adolescent years. The macro theory of motivation and behaviour and the now up-and-coming neurosciences are expanding scientific knowledge and about behaviour. Various psychogenetic micro theories relating brain development to cognitive behaviour in the neurosciences are also increasing knowledge about cognitive development (*Maslow*, *1954*). The neurosciences are closely related to explanations of behaviour disorders which occur during the process of adolescent development, in the formulation of his own identity and seeking equilibrium between his psyche and the environment (*Skinner*, *1938*). In growing importance are other theoretical formulations which explain heterosexual disorders (*Elias* and *Elias*, *1975*), such as homosexuality, drug-addiction and other adolescent aberrations. Adolescents entering into delinquent behaviour are said to experience conflict, frustration, guilt and other negative socio-psychological behaviour which create negativity in the growing adolescent.

We have rounded a circuitous framework of influences that are mainly psycho-social in influencing adolescent development. The adolescent begins to develop his own self-generated identity in an environment of factors which impinge upon his inner world of self-maturation.

Perception, Cognition and Goal-Orientation

Concepts relating to behaviour that arise from perception and cognition have their source in mental behaviour in the growing child from interaction with his environment, whether it is with the human being or with nature that surrounds a growing child. Perception occurs on the basis of cues that the child responds to as he arises from the environment. An infant, for instance, reaches out for an object that appeals to him, in terms of colour, movement and other attraction. If the infant perceives a red ball, he tends to move towards it and reaches out for it. If the nurturant reinforces this behaviour, the infant after many tries hold the ball in his two hands. This perception is carried over to cognizing the many varieties of movement in reaching the ball and handling it. He holds the ball, he throws the ball, he kicks the ball and thus expands the experiences around the ball and eventually other such objects that are red. He, then cognizes the many ways in which red items can be used and played around with. However, there are certain red things which are negatively reinforced such as reaching out for a fire that is red. He is thus directionally motivated by the reinforcement of the nurturant where he is not reinforced to reach and play with the ball or directed away from it by the nurturant. The accumulation of such cognition relates to the goal as perceived by the nurturant that as whether it is safe to play with or not to play with an object that has a red stimulus. Thus, through an accumulation of such experiences, he is reinforced towards the goal first perceived by the nurturant and then reinforced in him. The interactivity between the nurturant and the nurtured thus achieve many directions in movement towards an approved goal. The theories of behaviour thus consolidate the concepts of stimulus, reward, punishment, reinforcement and conditioning towards a particular response. Such theories are as indicated in the chapter on personal and social determinants. The theories of stimulus response, social learning, conditioning and reinforcement, topology, ecology, need achievement, psycho-analysis [*Freud, S. (1976), The Interpretation of Dreams. Harmondsworth: Penguin*] and motivation [*Atkinson, J., (1964), An Introduction to Motivation. Princeton, NJ: Van Nostand*].

However, the intensity of perception and the relativity of connectiveness between perception and cognition depends upon environmental stimuli, which may or may not be reinforced by the nurturant.

The Cluster Approach, the Priority Approach, the Dimensional Approach

The type of approach towards the stimulus-object or human

being may adopt a variety of types. A unidimensional approach is one where there is a direct relationship between the child and the stimulus, where the child is unaware of other barrier-causing objects, like, perhaps, a stone in his pathway towards the object he does not perceive and, therefore, may cause him hurt. In other words, in the range of perception, he sees no barriers. A second type of approach is one that perceives the stimulus as existent in totality and, therefore, attains a priority condition in relation to other surrounding stimuli. Further still, the child might approach many objects clustered together at the same time. His goal reinforced or otherwise is to collect all the stimulus objects on a cluster basis. The nurturant in this case directs him towards similar objects of the same kind which he reinforces as the goal to be reached. Thus, there are various indications of direction: the unidimensional, the priority and the cluster dimension, which become the goal-directed reinforcement by the nurturant.

Internalisation of External Control

During the learning process as the infant comes to know through perceptual cues about his environment, his perceptual cues are always changing as he relates to heterogeneity of such stimuli. In the initial stages, he child relates perceptually and behaviourally to whatever objects appear in his range of perception in an *ad hoc* manner. This depends upon the attractiveness of the object towards which he makes several different efforts. However, in the learning process his haphazard movements are redirected and controlled towards the goal perceived by his nurturant. This means that the reinforcement process directs to his own goals of attainment as reinforced by the nurturant whether it is the mother, the father, the sibling or the teacher. The whole chronological process is one of either learning about new stimuli or unlearning stimuli by negative reinforcement and be directed through positive reinforcement towards new ones.

Self Initiated *versus* Other Initiated Modes of Behaviour in the Child

The child is not a passive recipient of learning modes. He is usually selective as to that which appeals to him. It is only when he is in consonance with his nurturant that he, through the process of positive reinforcement, learns to appreciate what the nurturant would like him to do and, therefore, he internalizes that stimulus which is appreciated, which then becomes a set pattern in his behavioural cues.

The Paradigm of Influences and their Variability on the Variable Child

The child does not operate on a lone orbit. Nature has it that he is surrounded by different types of cues, some of which attract him and some of which detract him. However, he lives in a paradigm of heterogeneous cues affecting his behaviour and yet at times detracting his behaviour. He may move along towards attraction and the closer he approaches the object of attraction, the more binding is his behaviour towards the object or the person. This is the approach system which operates his behaviour. On the other hand, as he approaches an object which is not attractive, he tends to avoid and, therefore, decelerates his approach. This is the avoidance system which operates on him to detract his approach. For example, his mother may carry him around in a zoo, she might make gestures of fear towards a tiger, which he internalizes and does the same. On the other hand, having been frequently attracted towards his father, he opens up his arms and moves towards the figure of his father or moves away from a strange man approaching him. The child also moves towards objects that appeal to his senses such as taste, sight, smell and sound, and learns to discriminate among those that are pleasant and those that are unpleasant. Thus, as he grows and accumulates experiences, he gradually learns through negative and positive reinforcements from his human and ecological environment to accumulate those experiences which are pleasurable and challenging and avoid those events which are likely to be negative in nature.

Therefore, as he progresses in age, the paradigm of appeal and disappeal continuously changes. For instance, today he might take a great liking to bananas, to soft toys and yet in a year, he might change his liking to apples and toy trains. The nurturant's major concern is whether those items he takes to are good for his growth or not, whether they enhance his learning skills or deplete them, whether he desists his nurturants' attempts or takes to them. At this point, much of the paradigm structures also depends upon the overtures that the nurturants make towards persuading him or dissuading him. Since, there is a love bond between the nurturer and the nurturant the latter is more likely to respond to the nurturant's overtures.

Within this paradigm, the concept of need, its appearance, its intensity and cued movement is very important. For example, a child may be stimulated to eat an apple, but if after a time he finds the appeal of an orange more fulfilling that is he has an internal need to eat an orange rather than an apple, he will move in the direction of need fulfilment. If he likes sports, he may prefer to like hockey rather than cricket. His need is to achieve his best in hockey playing and eschews cricket. However, his variability during the early years of childhood may change as influenced by a variety of adults around him. For instance, if he has elder brother, who he admires, who plays cricket very well, he may change to imitating him and to playing cricket. If his attempts are unsuccessfully, he may give it up and take on to another hobby. Again, on the other hand, if he comes from a wealthy family, he might take to some of her sports which he can afford and yet, on the other hand, if he comes from a poor family, he may be reduced to playing "*gilli danda*". Therefore, children at different ages have different variety of traits, and this variability internally directs him to different sports over his adolescent years. Again, however, it is to be remembered that the nurturant plays an important part.

If she is a persevering and dominating type, he may follow the nurturant's directions and take to some hobby that is more to her liking and the persuasion of the nurturant.

Goal-orientations are many. How the child is influenced during his adolescent years to pick up one directive goal or another, is contributed to by a host of influential factors. These factors may emanate from anybody or anywhere. There may be a competitive fields of which factor is more influential than another and that which meets with his attraction. Therefore, one must assume, because of the variation of influences, the adolescent may change from time to time depended upon those forces which have the most strength in changing him. However, the strength of the influences may compete with the strength of his needs and often there is within him a jostle of different kinds of appeals. These appeals are relative as the adolescent is a male or a female gender makes a large difference in the kind of differences that appeal to the individual sex.

The paradigm also includes these differences that arise as to whether the adolescent is a male or a female. It is the usual tendency for the nurturant to reinforce the male child to study towards male professions, such like engineering, architecture, military etc., and if he is keen on sports to persuade him to take up a sport in which he does well and brings him a name. Similarly, with the female, the likes and dislikes of a growing female adolescent follow a regular feminine pattern which the nurturant, usually a female, tends to encourage and monitor. In circumstances, where there is a deviation between traits and hobbies, it becomes an intensive task for the nurturant to help persuade the adolescent along the perceived path towards the goal perceived by the nurturant required sex intended lines of nurturing the boy to behave like a boy and the girl behave like a girl. When the nurturant mother and father disagree about the type of goal-orientations that are suitable for the sex of the child, then disagreement leads to conflict and confusion for the adolescent in trying to find a harmonious relativity between his or her traits in interest and those of the nurturant.

REFERENCES

Atkinson, J., 1964, *An Introduction to Motivation.* Princeton, NJ: Van Nostand.

Diamond, Gary; Jacob Zalzberg; Dov Inbar; Zvi Cohen; Yoseph Laks; Diklash Geva; Tsach Grossman, and Herbert Cohen, 2001, "Birth Order, Birth Weight and Later Patterns of Growth", *Ambulator Child Health*, 7 (3-4), 259-67.

Elias, J.E., and Elias, V.D., 1975, "The Sexual World of the Adolescent", *Counselling Psychologist*, 5(1), 92-97.

Erickson, E.H., 1963, The beginnings of identity, in childhood and society. London: Hogarth Press.

Freud, S., 1953, '*Three Essays on Sexuality*', in J. Strachey (ed.), *The Standard Edition of the Complete Psychological Works of Sigmund Freud*, Volume VII, pp. 135–243. London: Hogarth.

Freud, S. 1976, *The Interpretation of Dreams.* Harmondsworth: Penguin.

Hull, C.L. 1943, *Principles of Behaviour: An Introduction to Behaviour Theory.* New York: Appleton-Century-Crofts.

Irwin, Altman and Joachim Wohlwill, 1977, *Human Behaviour and Environment: Advances in Theory and Research.* New York: Plenum Press.

Kakar, S., 1981, *The Inner World: A Psychoanalytic Study of Childhood and Society in India.* New Delhi: Oxford University Press.

Maslow, A.H. 1954, *Motivation and Personality.* New York: Harper Bros.

Piaget and Inhelder, 1969, *The Psychology of the Child.* New York: Basic Books.

Skinner, B.F., 1938, Behaviour of Organisms: An Experimental Analysis. New York: Appleton Century Crofts.

Skinner, B.F., 1974, *About Behaviourism.* New York: Knopf.

Thomas, R. Murray, 2001, *Theories of Human Development.* New Delhi: Sage Publications.

Thorndike, E.L., 1905, *The Elements of Psychology.* New York: A. G. Seiler.

Watson, J.B., 1913, "Psychology as a Behaviourist Views It", *Psychological Review*, 20(2), pp. 159-177.

3

The Psyche of the Growing Adolescent

The earliest form of the knowledge of human behaviour was psychology. Hall (*Hall, G. Stanley, 1904*) attempted to view the development of the adolescent in terms of Ernst Heinrich Haeckel's postulation that "ontogeny is a brief but rapid recapitulation of phylogeny", a theory that stated that the development of the individual is parallel to the historical evolutionary development of the human species. On the other hand, Hall's theory is a biogenetic one in that he says that adolescence is built into us, that it is hereditary and, therefore, not very susceptible to modification.

Psychology seems to have evolved out of philosophical thought and analysed man's thinking in terms of logic, propensities and instincts. These have undergone profound changes as study of instincts was not conducive to empirical data and still continue to have the type of philosophical sciences which brought forth a set of theories like those of Thorndike (*1898*), Pavlov (*1927*), McDougall (*1908*) and Freud (*1909*).

Bain in developing conceptualizations towards bio-sensory development used the basis of evolutionary theory of development of species from simpler species to higher species. Similarly, mentalism became the fulcrum of the relationship between the brain and mind as introspection developed inner thoughts (*Bain, 1868*). The left frontal lobe of the brain is responsible for speech and expressive language (*Damasio, 1993*).

In the study of human mind, interest in intelligence is of considerable importance especially in relation to adolescent, because it is at this period of time that proactivity can be said to be the highest. Creativity is related to intelligent functioning and intelligent functioning is said to arise from neurological factors, particularly from a distributed and integrated neural network comprising brain regions in the frontal and parietal lobes (*Richard, Haier and Rex Jung, 2007*). Such information can be garnered from studies of brain damage, tumours and the consequences of the intake of alcohol and drugs (*Dwivedi and Mukundan, 1993*).

Underlying the basis of intelligence are the laws of association, the laws of similarity, difference and contiguity in time and space (*Thorndike, 1932*). Arising out of interest in analysing these phenomena, the analysis of hypnosis has given rise to information on psycho-analytical behaviour of the human. Various damaged parts of the brain studied by the neuro scientists reveal that they affect appropriate cognitive functions, mainly in identifying the relationship between cause and effect. Brain damage also affects language development which is very apparent in adolescents who stutter and stammer (*Broca, 1960*). Das and Thapa (*2000*) have done an indepth analysis of the relationship between knowledge and its intelligent functioning, thus opening up the area of neural sciences in understanding how knowledge is cognitively perceived, stored in memory and can be deranged due to brain damage.

Cognitive development precedes intelligent thought processes but cognition itself is conditioned by the perception of the individual not only in terms of focus but also in terms of enlarging that perception to include other adjoining factors in the sphere of perception that are called cues, which give rise to cue grasp (*Markus and Cross, 1990*). It is understood that the more intense the perception, the more indepth it is analysed, and that it is expressed in outward behaviour as intelligent behaviour given the condition that there is no inherent brain dysfunction due to heredity or brain damage caused by outer and accidental forces. Perception is, therefore, a basic quality of cognition, which itself can be subdued, not reinforced, but can also be increased by positive reinforcement, either from inner dispositions or by environmental stimuli. It stands to reason, therefore, that if perceptions are narrow in its sphere, confined to relatively few stimuli and lesser still positive reinforcement, the potential of the individual tends to lie dormant. On the other hand, continuous reinforcement and heightening of associative ideas increases proactively the ability to cognize at a heightened level.

Thus, it is evident that, given a stimulating environment and a mental homeostasis, the individual, especially during the growing years of early childhood and adolescence, becomes more proactive and more sensitive to cues or stimuli not only from the environment but also from the inherent ontogenetic cues to grow in the realm of maturity of experiences. At the same time, there is no one basis for action and interaction of the individual. There are other factors besides those related to the psyche and the human world around the psyche. For a long time now, there has been concentration only on the psycho-social aspects of the developing individual, in this case the adolescent. As the ecological world expands, the experiences are decoded, rejected or memorized. Even the sciences of economics and politics are becoming part of the external stimuli affecting the psyche.

Heightened cognition among adolescents is a reflection of a sound socialisation process through which such adolescents developed. The parents either encourage or do not encourage the child to think for himself. The parents who do not encourage the child to think for himself/herself draw him back into a dependency relationship for interpreting the world around him. During early childhood children who have been positively reinforced, tend to explore their environment for learning those experience which are positively appealing. Such children tend to move away from the negative reinforcements from the environment in the course of charting a pathway for the future for themselves. In the technologically changing world, children who are less able to deal with an experiential situation that they happen to confront are at a disadvantage in progressing to the modern levels of achievements in educational and occupational areas. We only have to compare the educated urban adolescent, whether educated formally or informally, and his comparative rural counterpart, to know that the rural adolescents are less benefited from the modern technical and scientific stimuli than their urban counterparts.

At this point we need to expatiate on the meaning of the psyche. The psyche is the internal workings of the mind interacting with the conscious self and the unconscious self for what is called *'jeev'* which is specific to each human being differentially (*Paranjpe, A.C., 1988*). Further, the psyche as Kakkar puts it is the "inner world", the world in which the psyche introspects, speculates, picks up cues, discards them or rearranges them or builds up a pyramid of priorities as to which internal experience is more important than the others (*Kakar, 1981*). At the same time, there is a continuous dynamic flow of the thinking processes as they move from one experience or set of experiences to another. For instance, in the world of today, the urban adolescent cannot do without a mobile phone and talking to his peers. At the same time, in a different ecological context, a similar aged adolescent cannot do without either concentrating on studies or working at a semi-technical job or, as happens in rural areas, working in agricultural activities. The ruralite living far away from technological experiences knows very little about a mobile, while in the streets of metropolitan areas, there is hardly an individual of any caste or creed that does not have a mobile in his pocket or held to his ear, walking and talking. The world of the ruralite revolves around nature and natural things. Thus, we see the psyche is uniquely different in each individual, growing up on internal and external experiences, as they interact with each other to make up the specific uniqueness. Thus, we have millions and millions of adolescent psyches which are in the process of dynamic changes, which changes heighten awareness, passive awareness and as happens in mentally retarded children hardly any creative thought provoking experiences occur. The psyche makes up the individual entity which is at the same time protective of itself and at others covertly hidden from the rest of the world and hardly ever apparent to the outer world unless there is a conscious effort to do so. An adolescent, for instance, who is trying to be deferential towards his elders, is at the same time fighting internally to be independent of them, to use his own decision-making process, which he has built up within himself. The psyche is hardly ever in equilibrium with the environment. There is always a continuous adjustment, sometimes in harmony with the world around him and sometimes in disharmony, as and when he is in the state of adjustments. This very same adjustment process will find ways and means of being in equilibrium with the demands of the outside world, or at times in a state of disjunction with it. The psyche is not like a clean slate, for even the most astute psycho-analyst to understand. In a session with a psycho-analyst, for instance, the individual would reveal only that which he wishes to, and it is only after many sessions, after letting down his guard, he might reveal part of his psyche. The psycho-analyst might try to probe for more information, but it all depends on the client-counsellor relationship. One might say that the psyche of the individual is like a closed fist, opening up slightly here and there but never fully in order to preserve his identity of himself as he perceives inwardly what he is, as a human being, as a member of the society, as being well or ill-treated and trying to make his self-assessments on his own.

The inner workings of the mind continue to change as affected mainly by chronology because with the growing years comes growing mature experiences, or should be so if the adolescent is a normally growing entity. Sometimes, just one thought might be continuous in his mind. One might also say that this thought is like an obsession. For example, an adolescent might keep on repeating one experience like wanting to play football all his free time instead of studying. This is an obsession. Frequently, obsessions become so compulsive that they are not in order with the norms of the rest of the world experiences. An adolescent represents a break with childhood. He is expected in the social order to behave mature and not like a child. He is expected to take and pursue his responsibilities (*Murray and Kluckhohn, 1953*). He is expected to be in deference with the guidance and counselling of his elders, both parents and teachers, and eventually evolve into a young adult, capable of acting on his own, using his own moral self-judgment. One of the most effective psychologists of his times is Erik Erickson. In his book, Erickson describes eight stages in man's development. We write here verbatim from the most succinct portion of his description of the adolescent stage which according to him is identity *versus* confusion:

> "*With the establishment of a good initial relationship to the world of skills and tools, and with the advent of puberty, childhood proper comes to an end. Youth begins. .... The growing and developing youths, face with this psychological revolution within them, and with tangible adult tasks ahead of them are now primarily concerned with what they feel they are, and with the question of how to connect the roles and skills cultivated earlier with the occupational prototypes of the day.......*" (*Erickson, 1978*).

However, Erickson's analysis of adolescence at this stage is based on experiences of working with adolescent children in the West as a socio-psychologist, mainly dealing with analysis of behaviour and his inferences. His thesis is not empiricised as it is a collation of dealing with individuals in a psycho-analytics set-up.

Another clinical psychologist is Kakkar. His book the *Inner World* is an inquiry into the development of Indian identity. It examines the network of social roles, traditional values, and customs with which the threads of Indian psychological development are interwoven. In doing so, it reveals important aspects of Indian society, myths, rituals, fables, and arts (*Kakar, 1981*). In order to offer clarity to some extent of workings with the adolescent in his culture, we present here a vignette:

> *Shakespeare's hero in Hamlet was questioning himself as to 'what to be, or what not to be', as it is said in a nursery rhyme, "What shall I be" Shall I be a tinker, a tailor, a soldier, a sailor, a rich man, a poor man, a beggar man or a thief?" It is well-known that about the beginning of adolescence, the child, especially a boy, naturally turns towards thinking somewhat seriously as to what he would like to be when he grows up. It is not an easy matter, especially when parents think he ought to be somebody who he is not inherently inclined to be. We often hear parents proudly say "Oh, my son should become what his father is." In reality, this is often not in conjunction with what their adolescent himself think, for it is well-known that children are motivated to become only what they want to be and if they are pushed into a situation, they usually baulk. They do not perform well if they are pushed into a professional line that they are not interested with. In most families in India, parents do not frequently ask the child what they would like to be, they simply assume that "like father like son." In traditionally oriented families, the following of a father's profession seems to happen naturally. A businessman's son will enter into his father's profession easily as is evident in many traditional business families in India. The choice of a profession was not very difficult in the previous decades, since there were not many alternatives, but as social change is accelerating and in open market the Indian horizon of job opportunities for going into different professions are numerous. There is so much of specialization in these days. Not only can one become a computer specialist, but also branch off into various specialized areas of computer knowledge: hardware engineering, software programing in various specialized*

areas such as geographical mapping, designing, advertisement, art work and such like.

Previously when adolescents had completed their first college degree, they had the immediate opportunity of going into offshore programing and development of various types of computerized knowledge for the developed world. It is well-known that, for instance, a doctor in the US can do a diagnosis, dictate his reports and send the same to one of the countries conducting offshore programe and return the material the very next day all completed. However, these modes are changing because of what is called protectionism where there is a movement towards in-sourcing, not outsourcing. There are also increasing opportunities in different areas: in medicine, in law, in engineering and such like professions, so not only should an adolescent who competes to become highly professional undergoes an arduous task of learning the skills of a profession such as seven years just to complete the first medical degree, but also several years of specialization and then the adolescent is competent to step up the first rung of his professional ladder towards being professionally competent.

Under such circumstances of a long professional training, not only are the tasks difficult but also profession may be arduous. With the high degree of competitiveness in these professions, only those who are extremely meritorious or whose parents can buy their way into these professions that the adolescent towards the end of his youthhood can also hope to be completely professionally competent. Added to this is the reservation set aside for the Scheduled Castes (SCs) and Socially and Educationally Backward Classes, also called as Other Backward Classes (OBCs). Unfortunately, among SCs, because of their poor initial education, students are not able to keep up with the demands of these highly arduous professions, and so find it a struggle to compete with the meritorious. Under this stress and strain, unless the child is eager and skilful enough to earn his way through scholarships and fellowships, he/she has to depend mainly on his parental financial support, besides their heavy input and guidance towards the directed goal. In the West, this is not so since fewer children compete for higher education and professional programmes, and since there are several government programmes and funding organisations to give them financial support, which they can pay back over a period of several years. Fewer go in for highly professional jobs. In India, attempts to complete the highly professional course entails a great deal of borrowing of funds at high rates of interest and that too with difficulty. Most highly ambitious students have to rely upon such funds to complete a professional course. Finding access to such long-term borrowing is fraught with problems and, therefore, high-need achieving students need to depend upon long-term funding? Perhaps only 0.001 per cent of the upper and middle class of the population get to be highly professional and that is only if they are continually persistent. It is well-known from psychological evidence that high-achieving parents tend to transfer their ability and knowledge to their children, while most of the rest who want their children to succeed are unable to help them, and need to have recourse to indifferent tutors. The net result is that even if children want to choose their own professions, they are not of the calibre that would be successful in accomplishment at a high level task. It is not infrequent to hear a highly reputed professional father like a doctor have an adolescent son turn around and tell him, "I do not want to be a doctor, I want to be a teacher or I want to join the army" and such like. It is well-known that during childhood, when asked what the children would like to be when they grow up, they invariably said "a pilot", *"an engine driver" or "a nurse" and such like. These* are of course childhood dreams. The real world in India today, whether it is rural or urban, the lower class or the high class, the spirit of wanting to achieve to be something better than what their parents are is unconsciously built into the adolescent's needs for fulfilment of a career. There are several older people working in jobs who attend out of school classes only in order to get better degrees so that their prospects for promotion, for benefits and other advantages might increase.

So we go back to the original confused situation which confronts an adolescent and the all encompassing question is what should I be when I grow to be an adult and set up my own family and care for my children. Of course, at the adolescent stage the concept of family and children does not usually occur, but at the back of the mind is a vague compelling push that they can now become more than what their parents are, and much depends upon their own inherent will to achieve.

No achievement comes without striving. Indifference and dilly-dallying does not bear good omen. The parents require reinforcing their children to want to be more than what they as parents were during their education, but more importantly, the issue is that when they cannot push the child to work towards a profession different from their own, there is often a confrontation between the parent and the child. Many a time, adolescents who are pushed into a channel of learning which is not of their choice, they are likely to perform poorly. It boomerangs and reflects upon the parents' inability to modulate their children's choice along the line of their ability.

We see in the above, several factors which interplay in the thinking of the adolescent. The first one depicts a rich adolescent world trying to buy friendships which in the socio-cultural milieu of India is mainly a façade where poorer adolescents latch on to the richer merely for the favours that they can get. This is a common occurrence in everyday school life where there are vast differences between the poor and the rich children. The second vignette is more intensive. It offers a picture of an adolescent who does not know which is the best profession for him, given the fact that he is much dominated by parental and societal norms. Choice-making is much more difficult when there are many alternatives as available in urban areas *vis-à-vis* rural areas and, therefore, there is much confusion in the urban adolescent's mind as to what he should become in terms of future professional aspirations. These vignettes are only a few of the many that pass through the mind of the young adolescent as he grapples with the ever changing social and economic events in the dynamic world of change today. This is not often so with the rural adolescent who either attends school fully or is forced to leave school in order to find a job nearby so that he can earn to help the survival needs of his family. He either continues to work in his father's occupation or seeks casual labour. But two dividing factors are evident. One is the difference between the rich and the poor and the other is the difference between the older and the younger generation, all embedded in the difference of wealth and class which are social realities in the world of the Indian adolescent today.

According to Erickson (*Erickson, E., 1950*) the previous stages through which chronologically the child passes should offer a system of equilibrium where the child's internal self is feeling confident about himself/herself. There are some studies that relate to the building up of self-concept during adolescence. Jogewar's analysis of data from a study of 880 students between 13-20 years of age showed that self-perception was relatively stable between the ages of 13 and 17 years. For males, self-perception was at its highest level at the beginning of adolescence, which gradually decreased to its lowest level at 18 years of age, and then showed an upward trend. For females, self-perception was low at the beginning of adolescence, reached its peak at 16 years of age and declined to its lowest level at 20 years of age (*Jogewar, 1982*).

During the second spurt of growth which is the period of pre-genital development and the phallic stage (*Freud, S., 1953*), the adolescent introspects on his self-perception of his identity and also the reflection about him by the society around him. It is during this time that he is faced with barriers that tend to deflect his identity. He also carries with him the experiences of the past. At this point, there is a struggle for ego identity *vis-à-vis* the perception of others of his identity. The adolescent begins to look upon himself as independent from others, predominantly from his parents. Basic to the search for identity is the channel of communication between the adolescent and his elders as well as free communication between him and his peers. This also implies, the easy access of his parents to his friends in discussions on professions and jobs. Generally, in the Indian society, such interactive discussions hardly take place. There tends to be a separation between the adult's friends and his family. Thus, the influences on the identity of the adolescent are the various channels that he uses to communicate and to interact within the norms of others; contending with the most influential of them is his peer group and more so his closest cohorts or gangs, so to speak. He tries to ape what they say, how they dress and how they contend with the problems of adolescents, so that he develops a type of social security with his most immediate peer group. Previously, it was his parental and sibling groups. Now, he at this stage attempts to move away from their family influences and to build his self-image through the experiences with his peers, so that he can build up his own identity, make his own decisions, develop his own self-concept and formulate an idea of what he is and what he wants to become at adulthood.

According to Erickson, ego identity is more than the accumulated sum of primary school experiences (*Erikson, 1968*). The sense of ego-identity then is the accrued confidence that the inner self continues to have in terms of self-perception. When this does not occur, then the adolescent is not quite sure about who he is, and what are the directions that he ought to take in order to fulfil his future/professional aspirations. In this confusion, he might exhibit behaviour that is non-normative.

Thus, it is obvious that the adolescent is in an extremely sensitive stage, a stage in development. As said before, among certain tribes, adolescence is celebrated as an announcement to indicate to the world that the child is no longer a child, but growing up into adulthood. Adolescence is a peak period of development not only physiologically but also psychologically. At this stage, the adolescent has either to grow or finds himself under-developed in terms of standards that indicate both psychological maturity and physical growth. The adolescent attains his greatest physical height at this period and his voice changes and he grows hirsute under arms and chest and in the pubic area. In the case of the female, she develops breasts, attains a slender figure and begins to menstruate which is the beginning of menarchy. Thus, puberty is attained during this stage of both physical and psychological development. At this stage, the adolescent begins to develop his self-concept as a worthy individual in his social group. His concept of need-achievement either develops or stagnates. He also develops a sense of purposiveness or drips into apathy. Also, his perception of morals and ethics begins to mature or, again, he might not develop these traits. Most of all, he needs to assume an identity of his own apart from others. It is not that he should be "I" amongst many, but he should think psychologically that he is one amongst those who are of the same age and at the same state of development.

Positivity of thinking is an important attribute. Unfortunately, when adolescents are unable to achieve this fulcrum of positivity, they fall into awkward situations which they cannot manage. He may be in the company of peers who indulge in petty sex, who take to smoking and to injection of drugs, drinking, for the sake of the adventure or trial. His experiments often become habits and addictions from which extrication becomes difficult.

Attaining a self-identity is not achieved only by oneself, but by a selected range of those variables around the:

(1) Individual who reinforce their positivity on him so as to strengthen the path which he wishes to take.
(2) Most important of all, these variables are emanating from his parents, his relatives and social network.
(3) These human variables might allow the individual to find his own pathway or influence him along the pathway that they think he should perceive.

On the other hand, they might become overly vigilant parents monitoring the positivity of his growth and development into a personality which is positive and self-reliant (*Whiting and Child, 1953*).

The adolescent is very sensitive to admonition, especially in the presence of his peers. When his parents chastise him, admonish him, his self-concept of himself as a unique identity wavers and he begins to develop a sense of low esteem which is detrimental to formulate a positive identity. It is easy for a struggling adolescent to fall into bad ways and for this reason society reinforces parents to inculcate societal norms in their adolescents (*Saraswathi and Pai, 1997*). Communication and a sense of friendship with the adolescent by his elders help him to attain a sense of self-worthiness. Parents may find that recriminations might develop resistance and resentment in the adolescent and, therefore, particularly at this time, parental monitoring in a positive way is very essential. For the adolescent, the family around him is a security network. Watching blue films, porn pictures, indulging in petty and playful teasing of the other sex of the same age, all need parental guidance as there is a tendency on the part of the adolescent to hide these anti-social behaviours from the eyes of the parents and the world at large. However, it is not always possible to monitor adolescent behaviour since the parents are busy themselves and the adolescents spend most of their time in the company of their peers. Parents who are concerned about the behaviour development of their adolescents should, therefore, carefully monitor adolescent behaviour without attempting to show an insistence on the kind of behaviour they approve of, it has to be very delicately indicated and monitored, so that it does not enrage or shame the adolescent.

The adolescent is likely to develop a sense of guilt and anxiety as to whether he is doing the right thing and is following a behaviour that is approved by both his elders and his teachers and which does not come into conflict with his own needs and desires and with those of his peers. This is a difficult task and often sensitizes the adolescent to remarks that draw attention to him or her, especially about their physical selves. Such physical perceptions are of facial acne, over weight and other features of the physical self which are not appealing to the average eye. When adolescents hide their negative behaviour from their elders, they usually tend to develop a high level of anxiety and, more frequently, when they are competing with their peers, this sense of heightened conflict continues and he is anguished as to whether his non-approved behaviour will be observed by his elders whom he wishes to please. Parental and adolescent conflict happens frequently and the end-result is a sense of guilt experienced by both the adolescent and the parent since both are ego-driven.

A study has shown that the diffusion of identity and its relevant sex-role characteristics destabilise the equilibrium in the development of the adolescent child, both male and female (*Basu and Chakraborty, 1996*).

There are gender differences in the attempts at coping with problematic situations. Male adolescents entering into youth-hood tended to use action to solve problems, while females tended to find new sources of satisfaction (*Albuquerque, Rao, Rao, and Prabhu, 1990*).

A study indicated that when nurturants guide their adolescent children, the children tend to be high on self-confidence. In other words, the more the positive reinforcement of social behaviour by parents and elders, the children attempt to try and cope with their problems more confidently (*Ameerjan, 1994*).

A study to understand anxiety among adolescents in Kolkata city compared anxiety across gender, school type, socio-economic background and mothers' employment status and found that more boys than girls, more adolescents studying in Bengali medium schools than in English medium schools, more adolescents belonging to the middle socio-economic group than those from both high and low socio-economic groups and adolescents with working mothers, were all found to be more anxious. This study also showed that a substantial proportion of the adolescents experiencing anxiety perceived that they did not receive quality time from mothers (21.3%), and more especially fathers (32.1%). A large number of them also did not feel comfortable to share their personal issues with their parents, especially the father (*Deb, Chatterjee and Walsh, 2010*). For this reason many bright thinking schools have a section on guidance and counselling both for personal development as well as academic development.

The path that socio-religious norms play during this period of development is of great significance. Socio-religious norms teach the adolescents about the scriptures and other religious books, the learning of saints and the abiding by rituals. If this is not done, the adolescent develops a sense of hypocrisy and guile to hide the real truth from his family and social network. It is to be remembered that both the parents and the child have their own attributes which are ontogenetic in nature and are derived from heredity and environment. Nurturing is in the hands of the parents. Inherited characteristics and nurture is the influence of the environment. Both these interact in different degrees.

There have often been cases when adolescents go the wrong way. Deaddiction homes have many adolescents who have taken to drugs or to alcohol. Parents take children by force to these drug deaddiction homes where the attendants try not to force behaviour that is acceptable, but try to reason with them, offer those different directions and also anti-drug medication. Once a child has gone too far, it is difficult to think that if the child is in a drug deaddiction home, he is cured after a while. This is certainly not the truth. Very often the so-called reformed addict lapses back into the old ways and have to be resettled in a deaddiction home. This happens fairly frequently. That is why, psychological guidance and counselling is given in schools to peer groups to point out to them the irretrievable dangers of these habits. Unfortunately, such courses are few and far between and are most likely to be found in high-fee-paying schools.

A study has found that high need-achievement in adolescents is related to higher modernity scores. In short, higher need-achievement is related to a higher understanding of the various facets of modernity in the growing world of the adolescents (*Chengti and Halyal, 1995*).

In a study where statistical tests were used on high school students, there was no significant relationship between self-concept and academic achievement. Apparently, some other variables like application of the mind to the goal and a steady concentration on goal-achievement could not be readily identified (*Deshmukh, 1991*).

High achievers were low on neuroticism, guilt and inferiority feelings and had moderate concepts in evaluating their personal worth (*Devi, 1982*).

In a study on a number of social groups including the Scheduled Castes, it was found that the Scheduled Castes performed lower than others. This is an important finding because it indicates that either the Scheduled Castes themselves have low self-esteem or low ability to compete or they were not given as much attention as to the other ethnic groups (*Dubey and Mishra, 1997*).

A study on the academic achievement of pupil-teachers found significant effect on academic achievement of the three variables studied, namely, class room climate, teachers' leadership behaviour, and their expectations (*Gyanani, T.C., 1998*).

These studies indicate a variety of variables that impinge upon the growing adolescent's psyche.

The factor of social class also contribute in the development of the psyche. The majority of the poor have poor self-concepts. Again, the self-concept is raised or lowered depending upon the harmony in the home. In the lower socio-economic classes, domestic abuse and drinking among men-folk have their repercussions on the development of the adolescent, especially females who are sensitive and live within the home environment most of the time.

This affects the male children to become aggressive and even get into fights with the drunken father. Female children just cover and are afraid to exhibit their self-pacing in becoming well-brought up females, especially psychologically.

The search for an identity that is equilibrium between the adolescent's own self-worth and the approbation he gets from his social network produces in him goal-concentration to fulfil his aspirations. When several of these factors are in juxtaposition, there is family disharmony, other additive factors are: his need to avail education, to indulge in experimental ways that are not conforming to societal norms and geo-ecological and social class differences. These produce further barriers to the adolescents to try to achieve to become a well-formed entity. Thus, we find that the juxtapositioning in a malformed way affects each adolescent in different ways, in different combinations. Some of these characteristics bring about a highly negative character and other traits may be downplayed. Therefore, the personality of the adolescent, his heredity intake and both nature and human environments affect the adolescent in different degrees, in different situations.

REFERENCES

Albuquerque, Z.M.; Rao, K.; Rao, Subbakrishna D.K.; and Prabhu, G.G., 1990, "Coping Behaviour among College Students", *Indian Journal of Clinical Psychology*, 17 (1), 17-20.

Ameerjan, M.S., 1994, "Perceived Parental Behaviour and Self-Confidence", *Journal of Psychological Researches*, 38 (3), 1-4.

Bain, A., 1868, *Mental Science: A Compendium of Psychology and the History of Philosophy:* New York: Appleton.

Basu, J., and Chakraborty, U., 1996, "Effect of Sex-role Identity on Academic Achievement of Late Adolescents in India", *The Journal of Social Psychology*, 136 (2), 257-259.

Broca, P. 1960, "Remarks on the Faculty of Articulate Language, followed by an Observation of Aphemia", in G. Von Bonin (ed.), *Some Papers on the Cerebral Cortex*. Springfield, IL: Charles C. Thomas (original work published in 1861).

Chengti S., and Halyal, S.P., 1995, "Academic Achievement, Intelligence and Modernity", *Social Change*, 25(4), pp. 56-62.

Damasio, 1993, "Aphasia", *New England Journal of Medicine*, 326: 531-39.

Das, J.P., and K. Thapa, 2000, "Intelligence and Cognitive Process", in J. Pandey (ed.), *Psychology in India Revisited—Developments in the Discipline. Vol. 1: Psychological Foundation and Human Cognition*. New Delhi: Sage.

Deb, Sibnath; Chatterjee, Pooja; and Walsh, Kerryann M., 2010, "Anxiety among high school students in India: comparisons across gender, school type, social strata, and perceptions of quality time with parents", *Australian Journal of Educational and Developmental Psychology*, 10(1), pp. 18-31.

Devi, B., 1982, "Certain Psychological Factors of Adjustment Influencing Achievement among School Children", *Indian Journal of Psychology*, 57 (3-4), pp. 141-153.

Deshmukh, N.H., 1991, "Goad-discrepancy as a Function of Self-Concept, Intelligence and Academic Achievement", *Indian Psychological Review*, 36 (3 and 4), pp. 34-41.

Dwivedi, P., and C.R. Mukundan, 1993, "Lateralisation of Visual Attention and Distractability", *NIMHANS Journal*, 11, pp. 27-33.

Dubey, S.N., and Mishra, A.K., 1997, "Determination of Academic Success among Rural Girls", *Journal of Psychological Researches*, 41 (1 and 20), pp. 46-53.

Freud, S., 1953, "Three Essays on Sexuality", in J. Strachey (ed.), *The Standard Edition of the Complete Psychological Works of Sigmund Freud*, Volume VII, pp. 135–243. London: Hogarth.

Freud, 1909, "Analysis of a Phobia in a Five-Year Old Boy", in *The Pelican Freud Library*, 1977, Vol. 8, Case Histories 1, pp. 169-306.

Erickson, E.H., 1950, *Childhood and Society*, New York, Norton.

Erikson, E.H., 1968, *Identity: Youth and Crisis*, New York, Norton.

Erickson, E.H., 1978, *Childhood and Society*, Frogmore, St. Albans, Triad Paladin.

Gyanani, T.C., 1998, "Effect of Classroom Climate, Teachers' Leadership Behaviour, and Expectations on Students' Scholastic Achievement", *Indian Educational Review*, 34, pp. 34-39.

Hall, G. Stanley, 1904, *Adolescence: Its Psychology and its Relations to Physiology, Anthropology, Sociology, Sex, Crime, Religion, and Education*. New York: Appleton-Century Crofts.

Jogewar, V.V., 1982, "Development of Self-Concept during Adolescence", *Asian Journal of Psychology and Education*, 9(1), 3-7.

Kakar, S. 1981. *The Inner World: A Psychoanalytic Study of Childhood and Society in India*. New Delhi: Oxford University Press.

Markus, H.R., and S.E. Cross, 1990, 'The Interpersonal Self', in L.A. Pervin (ed.), *Handbook of Personality Theory and Research*, New York: Guilford Press, pp. 576-608.

McDougall, 1908, *Introduction to Social Psychology*. Methuen & Co., London.

Murray, H.A., and C. Kluckhohn, 1953, "Outline of a Construction of Personality", in C. Kluckhohn, H.A. Murray and D. Schneider (eds), *Personality in Nature, Society and Culture*, 2nd ed. New York: Knopf.

Paranjpe, A.C., 1988, "A Personality Theory according to *Vedanta*", in A.C. Paranjpe, D.Y.F. Ho and R.W. Reiber (eds.), *Asian Contributions to Psychology*, pp. 185-214. New York: Praeger.

Pavlov, I.P., 1927, *Conditioned Reflexes: An Investigation of the Physiological Activity of the Cerebral Cortex*. Translated and Edited by G. V. Anrep. London: Oxford University Press.

Richard, Haier and Rex Jung, 2007, "The Pareto-Frontal Integration Theory (P-FIT) of intelligence: Converging Neuro-imaging Evidence", *Behavioural and Brain Sciences*, 30, pp. 135-187.

Saraswathi, T.S., and Pai, S., 1997, 'Socialisation in the Indian Context', in H.S.R. Kao, D. Sinha (eds.), *Asian Perspectives on Psychology*. New Delhi: Sage.

Thorndike, E.L., 1932, *The Fundamentals of Learning*, New York, Columbia University Press.

Thorndike, E.L., 1898, "Animal Intelligence: An Experimental Study of the Associative Processes in Animals", *Psychological Review, Monograph Supplements*, No. 8, New York: Macmillan.

Whiting, J.W.M., and I.L. Child, 1953, *Child Training and Personality*. New Haven: Yale University Press.

4

The Influence of the Family and the Relational Network

A child does not grow up in isolation of the influences of other human beings. His foundational personality is moulded by the various influences of other human beings during the various chronological stages from infancy, early childhood and primary school years, into adolescence and then onto youthhood. The closest influences are those that emanate from the family in which he is bonded from birth. Throughout the different stages of development, the family, especially, the parents greatly influence the individual's development. The mother is the main nurturer as she cares for the child physically and psychologically, guiding and mentoring him along the pathway which she perceives is best suited for him. The father's influence is second only to that of the mother. The father, although not in constant contact with the adolescent, has a great deal of influence over the adolescent in the control of his behaviour, limitations and reinforcement. The role of the mother is generally called "the expressive role" and that of the father is called "the instrumental role".

There is a "gender difference" between the ways in which the male and female are socialized (*Omvedt and Geetha, 2006*). This is especially obvious in the Indian society which emphasizes the male role and de-emphasizes the female role in the interactions in the family network and in the society at large. This is because the philosophy in India emphasizes the patriarchal role socially, psychologically and religiously (*Bhasin, K., 1994*).

The root of these behaviours, attitudes and traits is based on the philosophy of socio-religious beliefs and related ritualistic values. The parents bring with them from their childhood their own values for childcare. They had been themselves socialized in a more traditional manner than they see in the present day world around. This is because the world is changing so rapidly that the children get more accustomed to newer ideologies than that of their parents which is more or less older in terms of ideology and behaviour. The reinforcement that the parents use is according to the goal aspirations they have for their children's future. These aspirations tend to permeate through their oral communication and behavioural attitudes in interaction with their children. Social learning theory emphasizes the imitative role model that the parents present to the children (*Bandura, 1977*). On the basis of this, the children tend to follow the ways of their parents, unless and until there is a breakdown in communication or a confrontation about behaviour and the way it is viewed by society.

These assumptions are made based on the premise that these are normal families living the way that is idealistic, where there is equilibrium in relations between the parents and their children and among their relatives. In actual fact, however, there are many variations. The child may be in a family where parents are divorced, where the child is brought up by a widowed mother or a new family where the mother marries and the adolescent has a new step-parent. There are also many families which are single-parent families. Further, the father may be working and the mother a home-maker. On the other hand, both of them may be working outside the home. Such changes bring about subtle influences in the way the child is socialized. However, by and large most families in India, on the average, live a normal family life. Yet again, there are many other extraneous factors like the influence of belonging to a particular caste, socio-economic class, a particular ethnic group and to the various regions of the country. These factors may bring about subtle differences. These social-psychological factors may change the image of what is perceived as a normal family life.

The most significant thread in the socialisation process is the consistency or inconsistency of interaction and communication of family members with the adolescent. Whether verbally or non-verbally, parents usually tend to set certain limits for bringing about discipline in adolescent behaviour, especially of the female. From a parental perspective, these limits are essential to create an understanding among adolescents as to what is expected of them in terms of behaviour, moral values like self-control and attitudes, focused attention and in the pursuance of a profession. When there is inconsistency as in *laissez faire* parenting or when there is rigidity as in authoritarian parenting, there tends to be dissonance between the adult and the child, leading to non-adaptive behaviour in the adolescent, male or female. This may lead to constant friction between the parent and the adolescent, especially the male adolescent. Such non-adaptability leads the adolescent to deviant ways of behaviour, many times unknown to the parents. This happens in all socio-economic classes to some degree or other. For, the child has his own ontogenetically developed personality trends as different from those of his parents. In a family, for instance, there may be a great deal of rigidity in the upbringing of the female child and carelessness in the way the male child is brought up, while in others the attitude may be the same towards both the sexes. In other words, variations do exist in the upbringing of the two genders.

Again it is not only the parent who socializes the child, but also the teacher and other relatives like grandparents. Frequently, the influence of the teacher might tend to be greater than that of the parent as often children are great admirers of teachers and tend to uphold their teachings as being sacrosanct even beyond that of the parents. However, most schools, especially for the lower socio-economic classes, have poor infrastructure and poorly trained personnel. Therefore, adolescents might not follow the best way possible when acting according to the instructions of the teacher. Again, in many schools, even the schools for the upper socio-economic classes, there is little in the way of psychological guidance and mentoring (*Havighurst, 1972*).

Besides these aspects of interventions into conceptualized normal family, there are extraneous factors, chief amongst them being extra-familial care given by interventionists. These are when the adolescent is in the care of other than family members. For example, those living in hostels are influenced by the adults who are in charge of such facilities. The adolescent is then exposed to a different environment than would happen if he were to be brought up only in his own family set-up. In the situation of extra familiar care, there is less emotional caring and much more emphasis on rules and regulations. These rules and regulations apply especially if it is a hostel or a boarding accommodation where the adolescent is exposed to a new set of values and rules, which then can be confusing *vis-à-vis* the familiar family set-up. The adolescent has to adjust to a new set of values, which limit the satisfaction of his own needs and subject him to non-familial disciplinary routine. On the other hand, he may be sent to a different family as and when parents are on transfer, and they have to move to a different locale, while the adolescent finishes his education and, therefore, is cared for by another family for the time being. There are many instances of the latter situation where the adolescent who is finishing his studies is for a time being looked after by a friend's or relative's family and, therefore, has to adjust to their lifestyles which is different from that of his own family. These differential situations create confusion and lend the adolescent liable to a sense of confusion and dissonance. For, in these various sets of experiences, he is exposed to differential behaviour and their effects on him in his behaviour. There are also situations where the adolescents, during this transitory period, may lose either of the parents or a sibling and this might further stress the already overwhelmed adolescent.

Thus, we see that the adolescent is exposed to many types of influencing factors within the human network that he is exposed to and thus in many cases he is forced to take hard decisions to fit his ways to a new set-up. As we know, a human being has his own set of needs and as he keeps growing into an adolescent and into youthhood, these needs get stronger and many time irrevocable. When an adolescent is exposed to different situations where people have their own needs there is much conflict and, therefore, distress in the adolescent through his attempting to adjust to the new situations. A need is a very strong factor in the fulfilment and harmony of growing into a well-adjusted human being and when this is in disharmony with those around him, it tends to destabilize his personality, especially when it is known that some personalities are more sensitive to destabilization than others and suffer a great deal of stress and strain. Where does this sensitivity to other human beings in his own environment emanate from? They are the influences arising from his foundational upbringing where he may have been exposed to either very harsh treatment and, therefore, develops an inward growing personality or he may have been over-protected and, therefore, expects to meet with circumstances which suit his own needs. Thus, the psyche of the individual adolescent plays a great role in meeting with the demands of others, their commands, and barriers to the formation of his own needs and their fulfilment (*Atkinson, 1966*).

Adolescent developmental tasks, as delineated by Havighurst, have been cited several years ago, mainly related to the physiological and the educational systems (*Havighurst, 1953*), but few related to the psycho-socio-problems the adolescents meet with.

Currently, with the influence of social media, there is much information on HIV-AIDS and deviant behaviours affecting the adolescent. Parents, especially, of the uneducated sections of society understand little about these deviances or how to tackle them. Neither the parents nor the teachers, nor the schools, are able to aptly guide and advise adolescents about the consequences of such deviant behaviour.

In the earlier eras, there was a close networking among various brothers and sisters in a family situation. In fact, many of them lived together in a joint household. However, with the advancing of social and technological change, while the joint family ethos still exists, the families tend to separate into nuclear families and, therefore, are not in close contact with each other. Some of them also move away geographically and hardly meet except in times of family crises or other such events where families join together, either in sorrow or in joy, or when there are special events in the family network.

As in other stages of life, the adolescent in this period of development, is motivated both psychologically and physiogenetically by his own inherent attitudes, traits and habits. His personality is influenced by his own inherent ontogenetic conceptualization of himself and the interpersonal perception that occur unconsciously between him and the other members of his family. Thus, perception also includes the perception of the family and how the family's patterns of living influence the adolescent's thought and behaviour. It is, of course, not difficult to understand how these occur in a normal family situation. However, when these patterns change, various kinds of elements enter into the adolescent's life.

As has been said, there are many children who grow to be adolescents without the influence of a normal family or a positively invigorating social network. During the crucial period of adolescence, the adolescent learns or he is forced to learn, new traits. Assuming a normal family life, his main bonding with his father is reacting to the father's authoritative stimuli (*Lamb, 1997*). In this process, the male adolescent, may, however, become a counter-face of his father's personality. He may be a very strict disciplinarian, for he may evoke much provocation that male parent might limit the lifestyle of the adolescent. With the female adolescent, on the other hand, while the father may be overprotective, at the same time he is not as nurturing as the mother. The mother is the major nurturant in her expressive world of care, concern and upbringing of both the sexes. If there is dissonance and arguments in the family set-up, where parents do not get along with each other, the negative reflections might affect the growing adolescent and may scar his personality. In such situations, the female tends to side with the father and the male tends to protect the mother from the father. Underlying the statement is the Freudian conceptualization of the Oedipus and Electra complexes (*Freud, S., 1956)*.

There are extremes, of course, to normal family living. It is possible that the adolescents perceive at this stage the infidelity of the father and the growing apart of the mother from the father. Or there may be some attributes of the mother which are not natural like her paying more attention outside the home, attending parties and neglecting of the children. In such a non-normal family environment, there is bound to be a great deal of repercussions on the adolescent personalities. There have been cases where the father is an alcoholic or the mother is known to given to playing cards and gambling, thus causing neglect of the children. Adolescents are very sensitive to these changes in their families, especially in contrast with the normal lives that their friends live in their families (*Vimladevi, 1992*).

As they grow up, the adolescent children become more perceptive and critical of the roles of the mothers and fathers. Adolescents see their parents as their protectors and their nurturers and, at other times they perceive them as having to be protected as in a discordant family. Adolescents are also apt to be protective of their parents' non-normal behaviour by making excuses for them. But, nevertheless, parental disorganization has its influence on adolescents. It creates a sense of frustration and insecurity (*Ameerjan, M.S., 1994*), which adds to the build up of negative repertoire where the home life is filled with negativism, where each one finds fault with each other and where there seems to be no effort on any one's ego to make a compromise. In such situations, adolescents try to find relief outside the home in the company of those who give them a sense of well-being, whether the waves of influence are positive or negative. Where the family atmosphere has obtained a certain constancy, it is said to make a two-way interaction between adolescents and their parents where they learn to give and take, to compromise and to arrive at satisfactory solutions to problems (*Geraldine, Barbara, Richard, and Laurence, 1972*). Where there is neglect and lack of care-giving, the atmosphere is *laissez faire* where the adolescent is allowed to do what he wants without much monitoring by the parents. Therefore, the upbringing of the adolescent not only depends upon his own inherent quality of confidence, self-esteem or otherwise, but also on the support or lack of support in the family environment. The home atmosphere also depends upon the reinforcement from the parent generation, where the latter are in charge of the whole system of upbringing of the child till he attains his own separate status of identity and is capable of looking after himself and perhaps also earning through a profession (*Harkness and Super, 1996*).

Further, a very strong influence is what social learning theory concepts tell us occur in the interactions among the members of the family. The theory states that the learning situation being the home environment, the child learns in the pre-adolescent and adolescent years to imitate the same sex parent. The male child learns from his father how to behave like a man and the female child acquires feminine qualities from her mother. Therefore, both the male and female adolescents tend to imitate the behaviour of their parents whom they most admire (*Bandura, A., 1977*).

The adolescents move into the network of relations, both from the father's side and the mother's side, and attachments take place at family events, and at festivals. At these get-togethers, a sense of the joint family ethics prevails. However, this relational network may also be conducive to disharmony, for in many cases there is jealousy, back-biting and negativism from one nuclear family to another in the joint family set-up, if it is found that some adolescents from other families are accomplishing much better than their own, and this might lead to criticism and lack of the capacity to appreciate the other's point of view of behaviour.

However, by and large, these interactions become lessened when families live as nuclear families with only parents and children. If there are younger siblings, they tend to be surrogated by the older children in the family. If the adolescent is younger than his siblings, he tends to form a close relationship of advice and guidance from the older siblings. In single parent households, the situation becomes limited to either only the father or only the mother. These households may have become single because either one of the spouses has passed away or has become divorced. In either situation it becomes greatly difficult for the single parent to take care of the adolescent and other children, especially if it is the mother taking care of the adolescent male or the father taking care of the adolescent female. Most of the time, these parents have full-time jobs while also caring for the children. Therefore, a great deal of anguish and conflict prevails. Since adolescent children are less supervised in a single parent family, the adolescent tends to be more sensitive to the need of the parent and, therefore, are more caring for the parent in their anguish and in problems they face.

On the other hand, when there is too much dissonance and quarrelling between the parents, male adolescents tend to run away from home situation as they find the situation intolerable. This happens more often in the low income groups as they have no other recourse for the satisfaction of their needs since the environment around them is poor and destitute.

Therefore, the picture of family life assumes many vignettes: normal, with both parents caring for each other and their children; abnormal, where one or both parents are disloyal to each other; or abnormal in which the father is an alcoholic or the mother is of a loose character. Such types of abnormalities bring about disharmony in the household which affect the children and family, sometimes even with parents being unaware of the traumas the children might suffer. Since the joint family system has attritioned, the onus is on the biological parents to be sympathetic and watchful of the adolescent's behaviour, but at the same time not to be harsh and unreasonable. In these days of hard economic conditions, parents are working harder than ever to earn a living. Therefore, parents are more involved in the socio-economic aspects required for family upkeep and less involved in the psychological effects. It is the lower class families and middle class families which are more affected by these economic recessive changes. Since the upper class families are miniscule, these economic recessive changes hardly affect them. However, this is not to say that they have adolescent children who are well-brought up, confident, with high esteems of themselves and fairly well goal-oriented. On the other hand, in these elite upper class families adolescent children have "too much too soon", and find wayward ways of behaviour which leads them down the negative pathways. Their parents can pay for their education, their trips abroad, their cars, their partying and such like high-class activities, little realizing that life is an earnest and the adolescent should be brought up in a straight forward achievement-oriented goal-directed manner.

It is necessary that the child's cognition is focused and limited to the tasks on hand if he is to attain a profession whether it is a lowly vocation or a high vocation. Psychologically his cognition has to be directed so that his activities are not deviated in several directions. At the same time, as said before, children do not always fall in line with the parents' aspirations and many of them choose to pick up pathways towards jobs which are easy in training and low in paying. As they increase in experiences, the adolescents decode the messages communicated to them and reinterpret them to suit their own inherent and innate wishes and at those times much altercation takes place between the parent and the adolescent. Sometimes, when confrontation is severe, the adolescent, usually the male, threatens to move out of the house and live on his own, thus estranging himself from the family nexus. With the female adolescent, however, this hardly occurs. Since she is limited in her geographical movement and since society does not approve of her being geo-ecologically free, she has to suppress her aspirations and is, therefore, in much more conflict and guilt-ridden than the male adolescent. Therefore, the female adolescent is more sensitive to reprimands and negative assessments than does the male adolescents. It is, therefore, the combination of positive and negative vibes that shapes the adolescent's psychological make-up. When parents and adolescents are in agreement about the channellising towards an occupation, there is relative calm and purposefulness in both the parent and the adolescent towards better achievement in their lives.

REFERENCES

Ameerjan, M.S., 1994, "Perceived Parental Behaviour and Self-Confidence", *Journal of Psychological Researches*, 38 (3), pp. 1-4.

Atkinson, J.W., 1966, *An Introduction to Motivation*, pp. 79-80, Princeton, NJ: D. Van Nostrand Company.

Bandura, A., 1977, *Social Learning Theory*. Engelwood Cliffs, N.J.: Prentice Hall.

Bhasin, K., 1994, *What Is Patriarchy?* New Delhi: Kali for Women.

Freud, S. (1956), *On Sexuality*. London: Penguin Books Ltd.

Geraldine Lambert, B.; Barbara F. Rothschild; Richard Altland; Laurence B. Green, 1972, "The family's influence on adolescent development", in Geraldine Lambert, B., Barbara F. Rothschild, Richard Altland, Laurence B. Green, *Adolescence: Transition from Childhood to Maturity*. Monterey, California: Brooks/Cole Publishing Company.

Harkness, S., and C. M. Super, 1996, *Parents' Cultural Belief Systems*, New York: Guilford Publications.

Havighurst, R.J., 1953, *Human Development and Education*. New York: Longmans.

Havighurst, R.J., 1972, *Development Tasks and Education*, Third Rev. Ed. New York: McKay.

Lamb M., 1997, "Fathers and Child Development", in Lamb M. (ed.), *The Father's Role in Child Development.* New York: John Wiley & Sons, 1-18.

Omvedt, G., and V. Geetha, 2006, *Patriarchy*, Lancaster, UK: Gazelle Books Services Ltd.

Vimladevi, 1992, "A Comparative Study of Adjustment Problems among Adolscents of Alcoholic and Non-Alcoholic Fathers", *Indian Journal of Applied Psychology*, 30(1), 6-10.

5

Communication of Values between Generations

A value system is the relationship between perception of an object or person or thing in terms of their worthwhileness and utility to the perceiver. It also connotes an emotional attachment to the object perceived and the attachment that the perceiver has towards the object which is treasured by the perceiver and may not have much rationality attached to it (*Bowlby, 1969*). It has a pleasuring effect on the perceiver to possess the attachment and not part from the perceived valued object, person, or thing. This simple explanation is, of course, inferred from several psychological concepts and social phenomena. As the world progresses from one decade to another, correspondingly, society changes dynamically, not only in the context of social change but also the technologically changing world which influences every individual differently. The adolescent in this dynamically changing milieu is also affected to aspire for much more than what he is capable of at the current time as he wishes to move along as quickly as possible in the changing scenario. For example, some decades ago, a youngster did not know the meaning of a cellular/mobile phone. Now even primary school children are learning to use this communication material constantly so that even on the roads, individuals, especially adolescents have, more or less, this communicating "mouthpiece to their ear".

Occupational mobility and technological advancement are two of major forces that have contributed to the changing lifestyle of a considerable numbers of Indian adolescents. For them, India is a dynamically changing world that affects the mode of their behaviour. This is more influenced by the increasing communication technologies and the use of improved ways of interaction, and is especially affected by the propulsion of contihually changing media. What tends to remain more or less static is the economic betterment, especially for about 70 per cent of the population living in disadvantaged situations.

These aspects affect the value systems in the generations of the old and new: those who are brought up in the traditional value system, namely the older generation and those exposed to social and technological change, namely the younger generation. A value is an abstract construct and exists only in relation to socio-economic norms. It also affects psychological interaction and inter-communication. It is well-known that this speech communication is limited between the older and the new generation. It is almost like a subtle tug-of-war where the older generation attempts verbally or non-verbally to impose their value structure on the younger generation. Over the decades, India has passed from being a feudal system under one regime or the other to what it is now since the last 65 years, i.e. a mixture of traditionality and modernity. The terms "traditionality" and "modernity" being abstract, are interpreted differentially by individuals, either young or old. The abstract terms related to democracy like "justice", "equality" and "freedom", therefore, assumes different meanings to whether one is old or young, rich or poor, or whether the individual avoids the interpretation or intensifies the interpretation. For example, the ethic proposed by democracy is respect and adherence to rules and regulations of the country. Some individuals might follow these strictly, others might ignore them and yet still others give them a negative intonation. For example, justice implies the same treatment for both the young and the old generation, but actually justice has many qualifications for both. Equality implies similar standards for everyone but in actual fact equality does not exist in terms of the caste system, nor the socio-economic groups, nor the standards between the young and the old generations.

In India, there still are the larger masses of the uneducated and non-knowledgeable living in static ecological areas in rural and tribal ecologies. We have in India a curious juxtaposition between traditionality and modernity. Traditional life-styles still continue in rural interior villages, mainly mandated by socio-religious norms, while the *nouveau riche* and the elite over-exaggerate Western styles of living to which they are unaccustomed but nevertheless try to imitate. At the same time, the middle socio-economic classes tend to imitate the behaviour and value systems of the upper socio-economic classes. Adolescents, especially those who attend schools where there are several socio-economic classes of the population, are confused as they see the variations in their own home-setting, in the school setting and in the life-style of the richer adolescents among them.

However, the pace of acceptance of change, both social and economic, is slower with the older generation than the new. The older generation feels secure in the network in which they have lived since their childhood. This is understandable given the fact that there is a tendency for the older generation to hold on to the existing values of childhood and their own processes of socialisation to which they have become habituated (*Misra, Srivastava and Gupta, 1999*). Frequently, one hears a parent saying, "I would like my child to have all the opportunities I did not have when I was growing up". It is the common tendency for even the low socio-economic class of parents to want their children to have a better socio-economic lifestyle than they did when they were children. Since new events happen in quick succession, even the old-fashioned parents find it difficult to follow the trend of these changes and often times, their communication to their young is itself confusing and translatable in many forms. It seems that events change so fast that living in their sheltered life and not having a world vision, adolescents hardly ever get to perceive these new changing phenomena (*Verma and Saraswati, 2002*).

During their growing years, influenced by the environment of their peers, their teachers, and even the social media, the adolescents attempt to have different views other than that of their parents. The old diehard conception that the middle and upper classes would like their children to become doctors, lawyers, and corporate professionals is now being eschewed by other more attractive and newer occupations/profession that are being thrown up by increasing technology. This is often a bone of contention between the old and the young generation as preparations for these professions begins almost immediately after high school when both parents and children begin to work on what professional stream they should take in higher education. For the lower classes, parents want their children to work in government jobs, mostly as technicians, messenger boys and such like. This is especially true of parents in rural areas. As we know once tribal children complete schooling, they want to move into urban areas to work on construction sites and other such types of casual labour which gives them ready cash which they did not have before, as compared to what would have occurred to them if they had continued to live in their old geo-ecological milieux.

The communication gap between the older and the new generation begins with small prohibitions and restrictions (*Geralden, Barbara, Richard and Laurence, 1978*). A study of Indians and Indian immigrants in US done by Shagufa Kapadia indicates that while adolescents experience everyday disagreements with their parents in matters related to regulation of behaviour/activities and interpersonal relations, academics, chores and finance, in India such disagreements most commonly gets resolved through mutual accommodation and adolescent compromise. However, among immigrants such compromise and cohesiveness is much less. More adolescents in India than among the immigrant Indians in US acknowledged their responsibility to accommodate parents on account of faith in parents' experience, respect for them (*Shagufa Kapadia, 2008*). This is understandable because those who migrate to other countries, live their childhood in them, leave their own culture and tend to adopt the ways of communication and behaviour of the culture in which they have settled down.

Communication is a physio-psychological means of interaction. Communication adopts a language format for interaction both verbal and non-verbal. Since there are many languages spoken in India, difficulties are envisualised when many different groups from different languages get together to interpret and understand what is happening and for this reason the medium of instruction is very important. We often find adolescents are well versed in Hindi and English, but their parents are mostly illiterate or have poor command over Hindi and, therefore, are unable to reinforce their children with the values they have inherited from childhood.

The phonetic conveyance of voice is to show the emotional content of the speaker. Communication is a very important attribute of the human being, for it carried with it an emotional content which adds or detracts from the value being conveyed. He can speak in many voices using many tongues expressing many intentions, either positively or negatively. A language is composed of grammatical formats, and these when used in particular way, at a pitch and tone, convey heightened emotions, either of the negative or the positive type. When calm and deliberate, he conveys a lightened emotion. The emotions that tend to interact in language communication are fear, anger, and happiness and in fact imply the feelings of the speaker to the spoken (*Bamberg, 1993*). That is why people who succeed at high levels in the art of communication go through deliberate elocution exercises so as to impress the audience. As the individual grows, he is guided into maturity to formulate his language in relation to the person and persons he interacts with. When he is speaking to elders, the interaction is deferential.

When he is speaking to his younger siblings, it is usually chiding and angry or pleading or coaxing. When he speaks to his boss, it is formal and rigid, but when he speaks with his peers it is relaxed and informal.

Among adolescents and their parents the idea, the tone and the intention are conveyed in a two-way communication. Parents wish their children to follow certain rules and norms. The younger the child, the more recalcitrant is the child, but the older the child he learns to take his cues from his parents' voices and replies in similar tone of compromise, understanding and adjustment or otherwise. But when the situation is serious like the adolescent wishes not to become a doctor but a painter, he dashes his parents' hope and thereby ensures a wrangle of high pitch communication back and forth. Communication is, therefore, not only a channel, but more importantly conveys ideas, experiences, needs, feelings and values, and in turn the listener may agree or disagree depending upon how emotionally close the listener is. Therefore, the psycho-social context within which speech is given and taken, whereby questions are asked and answers are given, make an important paradigm of an understanding relationship between the older and younger generations.

Each country, each society over the years has formulated its own language, its grammatical form and, in many respects, the idiomatic forms. In India, we have 22 recognized official languages, besides about 400 other dialects spoken by the people belonging to hundreds of distinct ethnic groups and tribes in a variety of regional and ecological areas. Given the vast number of sub-cultures, their society's views, language in communication such that others who know the language understands what they say. It is very different when speaking to one's own social group or when speaking to an outside group.

The difficulty of translation from one language to another is especially troublesome and knowing that India has people who do not understand others' languages, misinterpretations occur. Communication is, therefore, a very complex concept to understand not only in terms of this spoken language, but also its undertones. To give an example, if one were hospitalized in most hospitals in Delhi, the language that is usually spoken among the paraprofessional is not Malayalam; nor does the patient nor the doctor nor the relatives understand what is being said by the nurses, by the technicians, by the ward boys and such like. So, in a sense, within the hospital wards there are two languages or more, that the language of the patients and his relatives and that the language of the care-givers. Therefore, the art of comprehension is very important. In this example, people come and go, but in a home atmosphere children are brought up in one language and only learn how to speak but to make out the interpretations of the non-verbal language which is not communicated, but non-verbally understood and this happens mostly in the language used in the family.

We have spoken a great deal about language as it is the vehicle of integration in conveying ideas in accepting or rejecting them. But, there are other things, other concepts and constructs which are attached to education. Education is not the learning of A, B, C or D, it is the learning of a whole culture, of how to speak, to whom one is speaking and the kind of language one should use. That is why adolescents enter into debates and elocutions contests simply in order that they might express themselves better and become better orators when they move into a profession, where their tone and elocution compels the audience to listen to them.

Sub-societies after sub-societies use a great deal of language combined with gesticulation, while a great deal of others speak without much emotional display. However, it is not just the way they speak, but the freedom with which different generations speak to each other, that is more important because free speech, but it is more the freedom with which thoughts are expressed without inhibition which gives many clues with the hearer as to what the speaker intends to say. When speech is restricted, and ideas are not clearly indicated, the listeners tend not to attend and, therefore, there are a variety of communication gaps. These communication gaps are related to emotional feelings between the speaker and listeners. The less clear the ideas communicated, the greater is the misunderstanding between the speaker and the listener and *vice versa.* In the Indian society, especially the traditional parts of India, communication is not free. What is said is only that which is conveyed as a matter of the team like the parents saying to the adolescents: "fetch your clothes", "eat your dinner", and "don't forget to do your homework". These are short restricted synaptics. They do not indicate a growing freedom of thought and that is why besides being a learning experience, education should include the following:

- Free interaction between parents, children and teachers since they are all related to the same goal, namely that of educating the child.
- The exchange of new ideas.
- The attitude of compromise and understanding.

The attitude of compassion and sharing form the educated framework of an adolescent who grows in equilibrium with his family and social network. When proper interpretation of ideas and values are communicated and absorbed by the adolescent, he is courteous, well-mannered and socially integrated with his society. He learns to eschew being aggressive and overbearing, and, therefore, unconsciously, imbibed the values of his society.

Thoughts may be conveyed unemotionally or may be loaded with emotional intonations. If understood as such by the older generation, then this is accurate communication. But, if aggressive speech is accepted as being milder than what it is, by the older generation, then there is miscommunication. The same may be said of unemotional speech being interpreted as being highly emotional. Therefore, both communicative speech, non-verbal communication like nodding the head for approval or body movements like an adolescent's running after a room where a heated argument has taken place with the parent, are all related to the perception of the speaker and the hearer. Often, when high tones and loud voices are a part of the total system of communication in a household, this may be taken as a natural way of speech, whereas if the older generation is used to soft-speech, low intonation, this loud aggressive talk and behaviours is not acceptable and, therefore, leads to disharmony.

Communication is not only between the parents and the adolescent, but also about the adolescent children which, when they are talked about, creates a great deal of anguish among parents and loss of esteem. We illustrate by giving a vignette below:

> "*Deepak and Mini were the parents of two children: a girl, Mira, and a boy, Amit who were both teenagers in a high school. Their father worked in a high-pressured multinational company. Mini was highly educated also. She came from a family where there were plenty of servants and both her parents were highly liberal and informal with their children. Mira and Amit were already in bed when their father returned from work, and invariably the parents got into a slinging match of recriminations. These were about her being left alone to take care of the children. His retort was: "So, should I stop working and wash the dishes?" There, the arguments usually ended. Mini was worried about Mira's protection. She had heard so many stories about girls being molested. Although she decided she wanted to be a full-time mom for her children, she felt that her husband hardly took an interest in the children, their work and their issues. He was so absorbed in his occupation that, often after he came home late and after a hasty dinner he sat down to work again till late at night. She kept her pent-up resentment till they had finished dinner and the children were in bed. She assumed that they were asleep. They were not. They could hear the raised voices of their parents and felt very unhappy.*

> *Mini snapped: "you don't even know how your children are growing, the problems they have, and the sicknesses they go through. I have to deal with everything alone."*
>
> *Deepak, the father, looked pained and said: "I would like to." She said, "What would happen if I left them at home with you, periodically, and went to my* maika, *kitty party, where I can have some rest and recuperation." And so they sat, each looking helpless, their parenthood going through a phase of figurative strangulation. "Lack of communication can be confusion worse confounded."*

The days of the old were a smooth process. Children were born and lived anyhow, grew into youngsters as naturally as possible. They were looked after as best as most of the majority of the families could, who were mainly of the middle and lower class and had to struggle even for survival, unlike Deepak and his family who were rather well to do and represented a minority of the families in India.

In the majority of the families, diseases were known to occur frequently and if the child was taken away by a disease it was believed to be the will of God or *karma*.

Now-a-days, children are highly cued towards technology and tend to use technical language, like, for instance, "Mother, how was I downloaded?" They meant "how was I born". They tend to use sophisticated knowledge and to imitate the lingo of their gang.

In families of today living in metropolis and district towns, child deliveries happen through the use of sophisticated equipments. There are fertility clinics and several strategies to induce conception. Until now, it was like, as the older generation said, we have children according to the will of the God. Now, it is how to have a baby, when to have a baby and what kind of technology will help those who are infertile or wish to use fertility clinics when they themselves cannot conceive.

Going back to our story of Deepak and Mini, to have two grown up children was a big responsibility for them, and they felt guilty that not enough of parental care is being given to them. This is not an uncommon story. Many nuclear families experience this type of discord.

Early proposals of the linkages between language use and socialisation was made by Bernstein (*Bernstein, 1972*). Though growing individuals in every culture are socialized through learning a specific language in early childhood years, language codes differ between different classes of individuals. As stated by Bernstein, the lower class tend to use a restricted code, while the middle class tend to use both the restricted and elaborate codes for communication (*Chaudhary, 1999*). However, in spite of all these interpretations about language in a family/social network, much depends upon the personality of the Individual, especially the parent who has more experience than the adolescent.

Communication depends upon the type of personality one is talking about. If the personality has, through a process of social learning, has been taught to be vindictive and coercive, he tends to repeat such models of behaviour in his interactions with others. If, on the other hand, he is socialized to be polite and compassionate, he will also reflect the same in his interactive speech with his family and social network. In other words, the type of socialisation the child is given by the social caretaker, the channels of information that are used and the expressiveness of the total family to national and world events that occur around them, as brought to them by social media, television, advertisements and other such real life events, inducts the adolescent and his family into viewing the world in a wider context. But, as happens in the lower class families, mostly living in a rural far-removed place, information-processing does not occur and the adolescent lives a restricted and limited lifestyle. It is very important to note here that communication for the adolescent is spurred on by his access and success at education. If as is known in rural schools, in tribal schools and places where education is limited, the child does not know how to read and write fluently and so, as the child grows to be an adolescent, his knowledge is limited and so also his expressions. This is unlike the urban elite and the middle class who are constantly in touch with technology, who learn online, use computers and the variety of channels in his simple mobile telephone instrument which is the link to the rest of the world. Notwithstanding this, personality, by and large, is the largest fulcrum in the communication network. This together with the experiences gained of the outside world, the growing adolescent increases his language ability, his knowledge of events in the world and, therefore, his sense of self-confidence and his goal-direction.

Thus, an adolescent who is socialized from his early years to be well-knit with his human environment progressively grows up to be an adolescent who is perceptibly in equilibrium with his parental generation, his elders, whether in the family or otherwise, and his social network. The child has to learn to find a mid-way between his own needs and those that he perceives in his older generation. This happens through a process of interaction where communication is free and easy and where the family situation is harmonious. On the other hand, if there is inconsistency in his socialisation from the early ages, especially through complete or some pitfalls in his intergenerational communication, he either learns to be well adjusted or erratic in his adjustment with his groups, informal or formal. When he reaches the stage of adolescence, it is expected that he breaks away gently and willingly from his bond with his parents to become a separate identity. He, in a sense, is said to be mature enough to be a well-socialised adolescent. This is not an easy task for the parent and the older generation to interact with the adolescent so that he uses his own methodology to arrive at his selected goal, or is resistant and is negatively disposed towards accepting any guidance about his behaviour. It is to be remembered that we have delineated from the early chapters that each specific individual has his own ontological inherent traits and to mould and shape them through specific societal norms is a task that is a parental responsibility through the socialisation process (*Thomas, 2001*).

This can happen only if there is acquiescence from both sides of the generation to allow the adolescent to become independent, to develop his sense of responsibility, and to ultimately find his own identity. This does not mean that he breaks away from the older generation but that he establishes relatively closer linkages with himself and the older generation's wishes and aspirations. This does not happen very often, for the adolescent in trying to formulate his own identity often clashes with the older generation. It is through a sense of bonded love between the older and the adolescent generations where the adolescent moves along the guided channels of parental aspirations that he learns to develop the new identity and yet at the same time is closely linked with the values and aspirations of his family network and with societal norms.

REFERENCES

Bamberg, M., 1993, "Communication and Internal States: What is Their Relationship?" *Behavioural and Brain Sciences*, 16, pp. 643-644.

Bernstein, B., 1972, *Class, Code and Control.* London: Routledge and Kegan Paul.

Bowlby, J., 1969, *Attachment and Loss*, Vol. 1. New York: Basic Books.

Chaudhary, N., 1999, "Language socialisation: Patterns of caregiver speech to young children", in T.S. Saraswathi (ed.), *Culture, Socialisation and Human Development.* New Delhi: Sage

Geralden Lambert, B., Barbara, F., Rothschild, Richard Altland, Laurence B. Green, 1978, *Adolescence: Transition from Childhood to Maturity.* Chapter 1: "What is Adolescence", p. 1. California: Rooks & Cole Publishing Company.

Misra, G.; A.K. Srivastava; and S. Gupta. 1999. "The Cultural Construction of Childhood in India: Some Observations", *Indian Psychological Abstracts and Reviews*, 6 (2): 191–218.

Office of Population Affairs, US Department of Health and Human Services, 2013.

Shagufa Kapadia, 2008, "Adolescent-Parent Relationships in Indian and Indian Immigrant Families in the US: Intersections and

Disparities", *Psychology Developing Societies*, Vol. 20, No. 2, pp. 257-275.

Thomas, R.M., 2001, *Recent Theories of Human Development*, Thousand Oaks, CA: Sage.

Verma, S., and T.S. Saraswathi, 2002, "Adolescence in India, Street Urchins or Silicon Valley Millionaires?", in Bradford Brown, R.W. Larson and T.S. Saraswathi (eds.), *The World's Youth: Adolescence in Eight Regions of the Globe*, pp. 105-40. New York: Cambridge University Press.

6

The Influence of Peers and the Societal Network

There are many sayings that are well-known about parents, the adolescent children and their relationship. Some state that "when the stable door opens the horse bolts" and "the birds of the same feather flock together". When the stable door is opened, the horse, or to put it otherwise, the adolescent, whose chaffing had been locked in by the family, now feels the freedom to move out of the home environs freely. The peer groups who have the same tendencies tend to form close friendships and, therefore, flock together.

As the primary school year old child develops a sense of independence and self-control and looks beyond the horizon to interact with other people the first choice are individuals of his own temperament. However, there are several negative and positive causes in the formation of these alliances. The adolescent grows into a mode of wanting to be more dependent on his own ideas and directions rather than those of his elders. The adolescent seems to be more or less autonomous in the selection of their actions, as this is the pathway to becoming a young adult. However, as the child moves from the micro-eco system of his family towards the outer circle for meeting people other than his family, or the exo system, the first context of interaction are adolescents of his own age, his peers. The neighbourhood perhaps is one of the first geo-ecological areas where contacts are made. Since most children in the urban areas go to school whether they continue beyond high school or are drop-outs, during that period they meet with similar personalities with whom they find attachments. The attachment may be one of having the same likes and dislikes which is "unitary in format". They like the same sayings, the same movies, the same games, in fact the same leisure time activities and what is more, there is a harmonious relationship among them, and like the birds of the same feather they flock together.

Studies have indicated that adolescents who show leadership patterns find many such adolescents gravitating to be in their company and those who gravitate are called followers while those who are ignored are called "isolates" (*Moreno and Jennings, 1947*). There are other types of individuals who form temporary friendships for a time and then leave for other groups more attractive. More often than not, patterns are more permanent when they are formulated from early childhood during the primary years into the high school years and then into secondary school years.

Adolescents when they become adults and meet their old friends after a long gap find that the old bindings are still strong as it is said one never forgets an old friend no matter how many years have gone past.

The major aspect, however, is that the adolescent wishes to move away from the parameters of parents and to seek his own autonomic base, and so it happens that as the child moves into adolescence, he formulates friendship on the basis of similarity of likes and dislikes, in the same neighbourhood and, more often than not, belonging to the same socio-economic class. On the other hand, the adolescent might form friendship with what his parents would call 'undesirable characteristics'. These may be from the wrong neighbourhood or from the school. It is most likely that these unfavourable characters are from the wrong neighbourhood since most parents send their children to the same neighbourhood school as others, and, therefore, have an idea as to what type of children attend the school. However, all children who attend the same class need not belong to the same socio-economic class, nor the same caste or the same religion.

Further, there is a tendency for poorer followers to latch on to richer leaders in the adolescent group to try and formulate a membership with the leadership group so that their own esteem might go up and they feel more confident about their knowledge and attitudes as if they were belonging to higher classes. We give below an incident of the same:

> *The setting is a fairly well-to-do school in an urban area. Prakash was thirteen years old and Raju was fourteen. So, as age-wise goes, both of them celebrated or at least their parents did, celebrate their birthdays with pomp and splendour every year. They had more mechanical gadgets than they knew what to do with. Both came from small nuclear families where their parents were working in high executive positions. These two boys lived close by in huge mansions, had a retinue of servants, but did not have many of their own age friends to gang around with, for the simple reason that they were too rich and most of the other youngsters in the school were not and, therefore, did not live in the same residential area.*
>
> *Their parents used to rush to work early and to come back late and to make up for not seeing much of their children, they gave them plenty of pocket money, hoping that this would be a fairly good compensation for the lack of time they had with them. When holidays came around and they could snatch a few days' leave from their important jobs, they took them to luxury places on vacations and hurried back to their work. These parents did not know that while their boys enjoyed seeing new sights and hearing new sounds, they got bored in their parents' company all the time, for their parents spoke only of corporate work, money, trade and such like, while their children wanted to talk of the snails they had caught, the puzzles they had made on their computer and such like.*

One situation that is clear here is that, communication is less where families are small (nuclear in size), where members are few and where adults live in worlds different from their children with whom they come in infrequent contact. There are extremes of course. There are parents who cannot get home at times their children do. These children who come home before their parents are euphemistically called "latch-key children". In other words, they carry keys to the locked house when the parents are away at work and they come home early to an empty house or to a house of servants. It stands to reason that if both Prakash and Raju come from small families, they have fewer interactions with children of their own age as they did not have a large family of siblings nor a large network of similar aged children. Prakash had an older sister who was in college and quite taken up with her girl friends, whispering, giggling and looking at their heroes in magazines, or finding new creams, lotions and other such cosmetics to make herself look pretty. Raju had a younger brother and a baby sister and each one of them had maids to look after them while their father was travelling in the world most of the time and his mother was either at kitty parties or at the club or at the beauty parlours when she was off from work. Consequently, he also felt like Prakash that they did not have a big gang of friends and so due to no alternatives they spend much of the time with each other during recess at school or at each other's home. Were they really true good friends? Apparently not, because each will tell the other what their parents bought them, where they went to for their holidays, what they did on vacations and how much of pocket money they got everyday, in their attempt to out do the other. When they first came to the middle-school, they were new and did not know most of the boys around. But since they were neighbours and were in the same class, they held on to each other. Thus, we find that friendship patterns are usually of those where there is social class compatibility. The two boys tried to form different friendship patterns for a while.

> *Prakash went around with another boy Manoj who was a year younger than he and whom he bullied a lot, mainly because he could not bully Raju. Raju would not take it from him and they quarrelled frequently, so he thought he would make Manoj his friend. Manoj strung along with two or three others, and for a while they fawned on Prakash, making out that he was very good to them, whereas actually all they wanted from him was that he would take them to the canteen regularly and give them whatever they wanted to eat. They came from less economically well-to-do families, and it did not cost them much to pretend to be his friends. Raju used to tease him and say,* "Are yaar yeh log aapke paise ke peechey hai" *(they only want to be with you because you can spend money on them). So he challenged Prakash that if he did not spend that kind of money on them, they would drop away like flies. Therefore, another premise we can draw from this is that lasting friendship patterns occur spontaneously on the basis of common interest and common respect and not on what one could do for the other in terms of favours. Prakash took up the challenge and when he told the gang the next day, "why not you all spend the same amount of money as I do," they began to make excuses. Gradually, they dropped out of his circle and, he finally found that he was only left with Raju. As the saying goes, when the well is dry the frogs jump out. So, one can ask, my friend, who is your real friend? Is he compatible, is he likeable, does he accept you for both your faults and strengths, does he console you when you are upset, does he try to help you solve your problems, and does he always stand by you.*

The above are the criteria of true friendship. For, a friend *in need is a friend indeed.* No matter how long or how short the period of time they are together, they continue to be friends even when they become older. Prakash was thoroughly ashamed that he did not trust his friend's words. In time, however, as they passed from one class to another, their group friendship grew but only with like-minded others.

In a group, the arrangement is such that any one of them could be accepted as the leader. However, what are the qualities of leadership? They depend upon the perception of the group members as to who is the most admired for his skills, his problem-solving ability and their trust worthiness in each other.

Friendship is a complicated affair. It can be struck off any time. One can be a childhood friend, may be the next door child, going to the same school, participating in the same events held in the community. It is exciting if one is also a school friend, doing things together. The relationship should not only be one of just taking, but also giving and forgiving. No one is without some defect or the other. There is always some "chip on one's shoulder". Remember it takes "two to tango". Close friendship is usually a twosome, there can be gang friends too, but it is like 'follow the leader' situation, one very strong character person may make decisions which others follow, but with the caveat that neither the leader nor the follower take advantage of each other. Further, friendship should not be based on borrowing money from the other with no intention of returning it. For, neither a borrower nor a lender should one be *'for it begets both friend and foe'*. If there is no agreement on doing things together, then it is not a true friendship. Real friendship is a continuous pattern, for even after years of separation, friends continue to have the same attachment as before.

There is, however, a very important issue, namely do parents like the friends of their adolescents? Do they tend to override their choice and negotiate friendships for them? What happens if they don't approve of the friendships their adolescents strike up? These are million dollar questions, for if parents do not like the friends their adolescents make, there tend to be common issues of confrontation between the adolescents and the parent and the friends. This continuous confrontation tends to disconnect the child from the parents and leads to a non-harmonious situation where there is little rapport between the parent and the adolescent. If this disconnect is stretched too long, the adolescent may develop devious ways of doing things his parents do not like or know about, till it is too late. Therefore, it is essential that parents know about the friends their adolescent children make and there should be every attempt on the part of the adolescent to see that his friends are welcomed by his parents. Such a pattern is more likely to occur if the adolescents bring their friends to their homes and interact with them in their home situations rather than meeting their friends only outside the household parameters. Such home and school interaction could then foster the likeability of each other on all fronts.

Therefore, sustaining a friendship depends upon family support. When this does not exist, adolescents tend to sneak away to be with their friends who are not approved by the family, and tend to get into delinquent habits, like experimenting with drugs, smoking or even in indulging in pre-marital sex on the sly. It stands to reason that whether it is Raju or Prakash, parents' approval has much to do with the ability to nurture the friendship. Most parents have rather traditional ways of assessing friends of their children. If they are well off, and, more especially do not have bad habits, and again if they are of the same sex, parents tend to feel comfortable with the relationships their children have with other adolescents. Children do not realize it but parents tend to keep a watchful eye on the habits of the friends that their children make. Parents "keep a watch" in many different ways. They enquire about where the friends live (assessing compatibility of social class), or whether the friend's parents are living a lifestyle very much like theirs, and keep an eye on whether their adolescent's friends tend to indulge in non-social habits. *The eyes of a watchful parent are like the eyes of a hawk.* In many small ways they convey to their adolescents that the "friends" their adolescents make are not of the right kind: a kind of covert protection. They then tend to restrict their movements with those friends whom they do not like. Adolescents soon are able to size up how their parents feel about their friends and whether there is "likeability" or not. This is where disagreements start. Things are said like: "why can't I? He is a decent person. Why don't you look at it from my point of view?" and such like communication interactions. Then often a kind of hide and seek game begins. The major blockage is lack of free communication. Many Indian homes lack the spontaneity of free conversation between parents and children. Children tend to keep to themselves, and likewise parents keep to themselves, as a force of habit, as most Indian homes have a traditional aura and little free communication occurs between the two generations. In the West, where most arguments and debates are out in the open, a kind of value system of independence operates. On the other hand, Indian parents usually use a formal system of "do's and don'ts" which then unconsciously become barriers to such free communication. In most Indian communities, there is an unspoken way in which parents communicate their approval or disapproval of adolescent behaviour, borne out of early years of training, mainly through body language. The mothers of the male adolescents are very careful about how their adolescents conduct themselves in public to be well-behaved. Behind their backs, they do not have a clue as to what the tastes, likes and dislikes and even more importantly the problems that the adolescents face outside of the family sphere. There is a kind of show to face which the adolescents learn quickly to indicate to their parents how they feel, which is usually innocent and unassuming. Besides, Raju's and Prakash's fathers have quite different characters. Raju's father is mild and unassuming, while Prakash's father is loud and demanding. On the other hand, Prakash's mother carries on a slinging match with her husband, while Raju's mother just accepted her husband's tantrums as part of his nature. So, everyone in the family tries to adjust, or does not adjust to the other's characters except for occasional outbursts. Adjusting, adapting and compromising are key words in the family set-up. No one family constellation is like another, as the saying goes they are different pebbles along the shoreline. In this fast-moving world of change, parents and children are going their own pathways. Yet, families try to maintain as peaceful a life as possible, not only among themselves but even with a whole host of relatives. So the catchword here is communication, but not of any kind. It is communicating that is accepting, tolerant and giving.

Friends during the period of adolescence tend to be more in their company than in the company of their parents or younger siblings. Each individual at each chronological stage tends to find his or her own niche of like-minded peer group, and many of them continue even up to old age. However, the cliques of peer groups are not substantially positive for the members. Sometimes, as we have observed in the previous chapter, an adolescent from a good status household may find himself in the company of delinquents from which he finds it difficult to extricate himself. So much depends upon the kind of individuals the adolescent chooses as her or his best friend. It is not necessary that the adolescent should follow the leaders, or that he should be conspicuously obvious. Sometimes, a friendship group is so strong that each member will give up a great deal to help the other. It is necessary to state here that the pathway of the adolescent is a long intertwined one with others. One is that laid down by socialisation processes imbued in him by his parents. The second is the kind of information he receives either formally or informally, that is, either through neighbourhood groups or as we have illustrated before in schools which then form the 'reference' group for the adolescent. School friendships tend to be strong. The casual friendship in the neighbourhood may not be. For, they are not on a permanent lasting basis. But in schools, adolescents meet each other almost everyday. Therefore, bonds become strong. These ties are, however, mainly for the school-going child whether primary or adolescents. There are a greater majority in India who do not go to high school or do not finish high school. These are the drop-outs because of necessity of other demands such as contributing to the family income working in the family occupation or other casual occupations. Even if these adolescents wish to go to school they have no alternative since they belong mostly to the poor disadvantaged and lower caste groups who cannot afford the time or the fees, especially in these days of the overwhelming costs of living.

From the total overall picture, we have said a majority of the Indian children do not finish school and for the adolescent female, the situation is much more barren. They then become the unskilled and unproductive generation for the future which is a sad commentary of the status of the lives of poor in India since it is the young generation that has to be imbued with high standards, creativity, high decision making abilities, innovative and bio-technologically oriented in order to move the country at a pace in the modernising trend that is apparent today.

In the Indian society, socialisation is imbued in the child to attain a sense of getting along with others co-operatively. Yet, at the same time given the world of social change enhancing achievement orientation a sense of competition also prevails. This emphasis on cooperation has existed for a long time given the fact that the Cooperative Panchayati villages system has existed for generations and has permeated a general attitude of "getting along with others" and of helping others in their times of trouble. The sense of informal togetherness is a part of the psycho-socio culture of the Indian psyche. India is more a collective society than an individualistic one, and so the tenor of peer groups relations is non-individualistic (*Dalal, A.K., and Misra, G., 2001)*. In these situations where each individual struggles to achieve, there is a strong competition between the ego and the libidinal energy so as to be over and above the ego. However, the socialisation process tends to moderate this and to bring at a level the ego at line with the societal norms. In these adolescent years of interaction with the peer group, the adolescent has to cognize what is important and what is not to attain a level of competence among peers. Thus, as the child matures into an adolescent, social norms reinforce him/her to seek an identity within the family and within the peer group.

This is essential for him to have a self-image that is unitary. If he has a high motivation level, reinforced by the family, especially the parental figure, the adolescent is encouraged to overcome barriers and to move ahead. By and large, as the adolescent moves away from the family, he looks more towards the peer groups for guidance and emotional support, as frequently his inner cognition especially in the phallic stage of growth, motivates him to be like the rest of his peers (*Freud, 1990*).

The *dharmashastras* do not dichotomize the psyche into adolescent and youthhood, but assumes a steady progress towards a deeper understanding of roles and responsibilities and their performance, in conformity with family and societal norms. This stage, according to *dharmashastras*, is called the *Brahmachari* stage, where the adolescent learns his duties towards the family and society. This brings the discussion back to the idealism of cooperation and collectivity rather than competition against others and emphasizes instead competition against one's self to improve one's status (*Kak, S.C., 2000*).

The adolescent is not a "man-Friday". He lives in residences, in crowds, in colonies, in shanty towns, in far away villages and in obscure tribal areas. These areas geo-ecologically circumscribe the parameters of his living habitat and at the same time indicate the kind of society he lives in and whose societal norms becomes his own as he is a member of that group which is his reference group. These reference groups may be hardly educated, may live a life that is ecologically bound like fishermen, foresters, miners, agriculturists and even within villages potters, tanners and little petty jobs that subscribe to the needs of the villages. However, in most of these small micro ecological areas, the tendency for the adolescent is to move geographically from his micro family existence to the meso system of neighbourhoods, markets and other adjacent towns where his knowledge and information improves. Living in a circumscribed geoecological area limits the knowledge that accrues to him as the limitation does not provide for expansion of experience and knowledge. In fact, these cognitive experiences are like building blocks. They expand the experiences to further refine the cognitive construct of the object, thing or person. For example, an adolescent who works in a tannery needs to go with his father to an adjacent village to buy tanning materials. There he meets others that are not tanners, but are involved in jobs like artistry, construction work, weaving clothes, or some form which is different from his own family occupation. These cognitive experiences are imaged in his mind and stored in memory. Each image tends to evoke more curiosity about how weaving takes place and how bricks are made and such like widening information. His cognitive map thus increases. As the adolescent moves further geo-ecologically, he goes into towns. He gets attracted by the types of technical and vocational education available and, therefore, attempts to learn by taking training classes. If he is a creative adolescent, he may grow up to accumulate refined skills and he may venture into the business of selling and buying, and thus become commercially attuned. Further still, these adolescents may get into business with people from other countries who come to purchase those items which sell well in their own countries. Therefore, we find that this adds to what is known as World Trade Organisation ambiance. Today, there are many rich countries that do offshore work with less developed countries. Thus, offering many youngsters in these less developed countries fairly well-paid jobs. So, we see that the youngster moves from the micro to the macro level of ecological interactions and thus may move into world trade. India, a couple of decades ago, has taken quantum leaps in affording everything that can be bought from abroad and it is astonishing how quickly the Indian mind in his corporate world has produced all kinds of goods which are available in other countries. Necessarily, this has made those at the lowest rung, namely, the lower socio-economic classes, want to compete and do better. The major incentives are social media and the world around them. Cloistered in little villages and in far-off forests does not present such a scenario to the adolescent of these geoecological areas unless they are exposed to the meso, exo and macro level of interaction. Otherwise, they continue to live the same existence as did their forefathers.

Are the friends that an adolescent makes approved of by his parents? Do the parents have enough time to see these friends, to approve or disapprove of them? Many a time, parents are so busy working; they only pass glances at the friends of their children, hardly enquiring about their backgrounds. The children of wealthy parents, as we have just indicated in the previous pages, are under the false assumption that they can buy friendship. Friends are formed on the basis of commitment to each other through thick and thin.

There is no way of knowing who becomes whose friend? An economically poor adolescent may become a good friend of a rich adolescent. A rich adolescent may discard the friendship of a richer friend simply because their personalities clash. So, when we try to match friendship with friendship, there are many variables which have to be taken into account and mostly because there is a liking or disliking between adolescents, the most likely being a rapport between likely friends.

Moving out of the micro-ecology of the family to friendship patterns outside family circle, special vigilance is called for on the part of parents, which may occur or not occur. Much depends on the harmony, the compromise and the interactive patterns of understanding and communication that keeps his patterns of interaction alive. While parents need to monitor her adolescent's behaviour, parents cannot be too authoritarian or too limiting for the child growing into a young adult, may resent such strictures and in fact may obstinately turn the other way and deliberately disobey imposed limitations. Values are instilled from early childhood such as respecting elders, valuing the social norms, which the parents instil in them and respecting their limitations and their disciplinary techniques which are not harsh or too demanding. Thus, the interaction between the parents and their adolescents in respect of their peer group formation is one that is of a compromise, communication and acceptance. What do these three values called which binds them together. These are learned by imitation during early childhood from their parents. The communication between parent and child is the fulcrum of a bonding that does not break for it is like a tree growing roots into the lives of both the parents and adolescents. This is also, therefore, a question of mutual trust and respect where the parent can trust the child implicitly in the friendship he or she keeps and so-called friends he or she moves with or moves away from.

REFERENCES

Dalal, A. K., and Misra, G., 2001, "Social Psychology in India: Evolution and Emerging Trends. In A.K. Dalal, and G. Misra (eds.), *New Directions in Indian Psychology: Social Psychology*, 19–52. New Delhi: Sage.

Freud, S., 1990 (ed. by James Strachey). *The Ego and the Id*. New York: W. Norton & Co.

Kak, S.C. 2000. "On Understanding Ancient Indian Science", in A.K. Raina, B.N. Patnaik, M. Chaddha (eds), *Science and Tradition*, pp. 83-108. Shimla: Indian Institute of Advanced Study.

Moreno, J., and H.H. Jennings. 1947. "Sociometric Control Studies of Grouping and Regrouping", *Sociometry Monographs*, 7.

7

Heterosexual Relations in Adolescence

Heterosexual relationships are not simply a male-female affair. There are several intricate and intervening variables depending upon the foundational bases on which the two sexes have been socialized. Such variations depend on whether the foundation is based on the values of traditional society, or on a modernising society, or, further still, on an ultramodern society. Unique dynamic societal norms also operate whether it is a tribal or rural society or an urban society. It is also probable that there are intermixes of all these types. For instance, in a tribal area male-female relationships depend on the structure and systems utilized in the special tribal framework. Sometimes, the relationships are loosely defined, as for instance polygamy in a society or whether monogamy prevails as in other tribal societies. A modernising society is a mixture of both traditionality and modernity in varying degrees. However, modernity usually implies following an ethos that is social and legal. It also implies being democratic, forward looking and accepting of changes in technology and new social structures as also adhering to their parameters. As for instance, the differences to be found between tribals living in urban slums *vis-à-vis* their natural habitat. India is not only heterogeneous, it is composed of large number of ethnic groups, religious groups and caste groups, all living in specific diverse ecologies, but in adjacent societal patterns such as the difference between an urban slum and elitist living side by side as seen in tall rised building structures, where the labourer and the builder work side by side. In cities, especially, metropolis areas, patterns of living are often free and unrestricted and more so for males. We have only to open up the *Hindustan Times* newspaper and see its marriage advertisement columns to be floored with the many sub-divisions that are asked for in the advertisements. Some even go bisect caste differences and ask for specific sub-castes. So much so that it is hard to synchronise anyone of the patterns and describe them as if they are representative of each and every sub-society. There are also on-line advertisements of marriage organisations which promise to bring to the enquiring person the exact specifications of the marriage partner required. Notwithstanding all these, there are usually what are called "chat lines" over the internet, where friendships are cemented for further heterosexual bonds. Yet, in interior rural areas and villages, the marriage negotiators perform their usual tasks of going from one family to another to find marriage aged children to whose parents they speak and so they contribute to what is called the vast array of arranged marriages. Surprisingly even in urban cities in the middle and upper classes marriages take place without the male even interacting with the female partners before the marriage.

Entrance into heterosexual relationships is usually fraught with many issues. These issues are:

(1) Self-choice which does not meet the parental choice.
(2) Attempting to marry a person that is not of one's caste or creed or ones socio-economic class.
(3) Thinking about marriage when one is still young and has not been able to obtain an independent job and not responsible for taking care of a family.

If the above are disjointed, the adolescent then is confused and is plagued between many divergent expectations. Part of the reason is that adolescents are not given adequate understanding about sexual relationships either from their parental nexus which is usually formal, where parents are usually reluctant to discuss these, nor do high schools undertake to thoroughly explain the meaning and consequences of sexual relationships as schools generally concentrate mainly on the physiological reproductive system.

However, before all these variations and relationships can take place, there are several concepts about the two sexes which ought to be known. The fundamental ones are self-concept, self-esteem, self-decision-making and the degree of self-control.

(a) **Self-concept:** It is an innate image which the adolescent has about himself or herself. This implies a build up within the adolescent of a positive or negative self-image. It is commonly seen when chronologically primary school aged children begin to develop masculine or feminine qualities in male and female respectively. Many of these self-images depend upon self-confidence and a high degree of motivation to achieve.

(b) **Self-esteem:** It is the degree to which one has a positive identity of oneself. Therefore, esteem of the self can either be at a high or low level. If the latter, the adolescent is unable to make firm choices or to arrive at decisive plans. Many growing adolescents, especially at the initial stages of adolescence, are not very sure of their personality pattern in the eyes of the opposite sex and, therefore, tend fairly often to be withdrawn, hesitant and unable to enter into deliberate and meaningful conversations. They tend to be isolated as in Moreno's sociometric analysis (*Moreno, J.W., 1977*). This pattern of hesitancy and shying away from bold conversations is more observable in female adolescents who tend to be hesitant and withdrawn in the presence of the opposite sex.

(c) **Self-decision making**: As the adolescent grows and mixes with several individuals in his immediate community in school system and among peers, he is likely to come across many experiences. Some of them compromising, some of the confronting and some others to which the adolescent is unable to respond firmly and with a decisive attitude. Decision-making is based on the individual's confidence of his information systems and repertoire. These experiences he should repeatedly attempt to understand to explicate and be unhesitant and sure about his responses to a debatable situation. Decision-making is one of the strongest attributes of identity-formation. An individual weighs the pros and cons and selects a path of which he is confident. Therefore, confidence building in one sense is essential to accurate decision-making.

(d) **Self-control:** The growing adolescent meets with many different types of individuals, some of whom he is inevitably disposed towards and some of which he compromises with and some which he accepts wholehearted support. The attribute of self-control is not easily acquired. It depends upon the high cognitive cue-grasp of totality of perspectives about the issues and even consulting elders as to what would be the best decision to make. This happens frequently in the selection of a plan of action for his future goals, especially professional goals. For this reason, decision making must have a perspective, a pathway and a goal related motivated direction.

These attributes are found in different degrees in different people and even among different ecologies. However, by and large, societal norms are the prevailing and fundamental influences on the individual adolescent. In rural and tribal areas, the systems that are formed have been laid down since generations. And, most adolescents do not side-track the norms of their rural and tribal ecologies. Perhaps, few of them get an opportunity to move out of the circular structure and age-old systems to find other new avenues, except if they leave their place of origin and go to another ecology like townships, cities, seeking jobs that are of casual and intermittent. However, among those who have opportunities to rise from their original habitat, they tend to be more in control of themselves and do not often deviate from their set goals as they would tend to break down the sense of self-identity. If we hypothesise which of these attributes are stronger in the male *vis-à-vis* the female, it becomes obvious that males are more decision-making in their personality characteristics that they have more self-esteem, but perhaps less self-controlled when dealing with the opposite sex. While here are no firm data to assess the differences between the two sexes in their attitudes towards life and towards goal-orientation, there is some supposition that males are more determined and more focused in their goal orientation as it becomes incumbent upon them to concentrate on looking for jobs and professions as they are supposed to be ready for the upbringing of a family. If male approach the opposite sex and they are shirked away, they tend to lose the sense of self-esteem and feel that they are inadequate to achieve their goals which is to be admired and approved by the females with whom they come in contact. However, there is no one to one relationship among these four characteristics. We have recounted that sometimes the females have a better decision-making imagery in contrast to the male adolescent and more often than not, they build up a sense of self-esteem that impels them along their own pathway. Therefore, compatibility in these four psycho-dynamic attributes is essential for a male-female relationship, whether platonic or sex-engendered.

At any one time, heterosexual relationships are hard to pinpoint and describe except in a discrete fashion and one can only make deductions on the basis of observations. This is more clearly observable in schools where high school males and females tend to form their own clutches *vis-à-vis* the opposite sex.

Among these attributes, self-control is perhaps the basic premise of a heterosexual relationship. Heterosexual relations can range from just platonic friendship to the two sexes being madly in love with each other to the extent of wanting to elope or get married even without parental consent. The real fact of the situation is that it is necessary to understand those ecologies, the economies and the societies in which these adolescents are socialized (*Saraswathi, 1999*). It is necessary to understand the chronological growing pattern of the adolescent of the genders.

The Physiological and Emotional Changes that take place in Adolescents

The spurts of growth during adolescence is the gradual reformulation of the physiology of the body. This spurt is manifested in changes in height and weight, hirsute appearance and voice changes in the male, and in the female bodily changes such as development of breasts and significant changes in other parts of the body due to the effect of menarche. These distinguishing features appear during the chronological stage of adolescence beginning anywhere from 12 years through 18 or 19.

During the latter primary school stage, there is often a relationship that is known as puppy love where young males admire their female teachers and the young females admire male teachers. At about that time when there is admiration for the adult male by the female student and *vice versa* for the adult female by the male student, hormonic changes take place. The androgenic cells develop more rapidly during this period for the males and the female develops physiological changes in her body and attains menarchy. As a child nears puberty, a gland in the brain, called the pituitary gland, increases the secretion of a hormone called follicle-stimulating hormone (FSH). This hormone then causes additional effects. In females, FSH activates the ovaries to start producing estrogen. In males, FSH causes sperm to develop (*Foresta, Bettella, Ferlin, Garolla, and Rossato, 1998*). These physiological developing phenomena differentiate between the male and the female. The formation and undeterred development of these characteristics, both physiological and genital need to go hand in hand to give to the growing adolescent the wherewithal to be able to deal with his/her environment, both sociological as well as physiological. In these days of growing social changes, there seems to be an increasing laxity in the monitoring of the heterosexual behaviour of children, especially among the middle and upper class. Unfortunately, secretive abortion clinics exist and if the female child is pregnant, she is usually helped by her partner to go to such abortion clinics which are dangerous and tend to harm the normal fertility processes in the female.

In the lower classes, we have observed where they have been love-pacts between the male and female not having much privacy to meet in their homes or in cloistered spaces, they tend to use parks and gardens, especially those which are highly wooded, for meeting and mating. In fact, heterosexual relations are not what they used to be in the bygone decades. There were strict controls on female meeting males and they only met mostly at the time of marriage negotiations. Now-a-days, in the upper middle and elite groups, the lackadaisical parents let their adolescents to be non-monitored and unsupervised. For this reason, the adolescents in this milieu tends to be confused, not knowing whether he or she should follow traditional norms or move forward boldly on his own decisions and roles irrespective of the traits of traditionalism with which he had grown up with.

In males, it is difficult to know exactly when puberty is coming. There are changes that occur, but they occur gradually and over a period of time, rather than as a single event.

Female adolescents experience puberty as a sequence of events, but their pubertal changes usually begin before the males of the same age. Each female is different and may progress through these changes differently.

At the same time, the sexes become aware of the differences between themselves and are psychologically affected by observation of these changes. Females become reticent or quite shy. Males become boisterous, aggressive and act in a macho fashion. Males and females are attracted to each other. This heterosexual attraction affects the two sexes differently. The girl is aware that she can be attractive to the opposite sex and consciously tries and exaggerates her feminine attributes. The male exhibits macho tendencies, that is, display of manliness, vigour and bravery. These characteristics appear in different degrees during the years of adolescence. These tendencies appear most obviously during the high school years.

Given the social structure and the systems of inter-relationships permitted by the society, each unique society has its own norms about heterosexual behaviour. In some tribal areas, males and females are allowed to interact heterosexually earlier than the adult years. Pre-marital relationships are practiced freely during the early adolescent years. Polygyny is found among the Naga tribes, the Gond, the Baiga, the Toda, the Lushai and most of the Proto-Australoid tribes of middle India. The system of women having more than one husband is called polyandry and this is practised by many tribes living in the Himalayan tract of India stretching from Kashmir to Assam such as the Tiyan, the Toda, the Kota, the Khasa and the Ladakhi Bota. It is popular among the Tibetan tribes living in Ladakh region of India and such societies are known as polyandrous. In some of them, free pre-marital sex is also permitted (*J.P. Singh Rana, 1998*).

Societal norms in other societies about adolescent sexual behaviour is strictly monitored, especially in the current modern day world. In fact, if it is found that if a girl's hymen is broken even though un knowingly, she is suspected of having had pre-marital sex (*Jejeebhoy, S., 1998*). In some extreme cases as in Ethiopia, Sudan and in some Arab countries, female circumcision is performed in the early years so that the females' erogenous emotions are curtailed (*WHO, 2012)*. It is not unusual that both sexes practise masturbation during adolescence and is commonly accepted. But since these are against societal norms, they are done secretly and is the matter of shame if discovered. These norms of vigilants are usually practised in rural areas and traditional families, whether urban or rural. However, given the fact that modernisation is gradually been accepted as a way of life, heterosexual relations occur fairly frequently, but secretively, in the adolescent years. However, the society has not as yet condoned pre-marital sex although in the upper socio-economic classes "live-in" partnerships occur more frequently, and while it is not socially acceptable, it is ignored. The tendency towards liberal heterosexual relations is spurred by suggestive advertisements in social media, movies and reality shows, where much of the attractiveness of the male and female bodies are revealed seductively so that they stimulate the erogenous emotions of the young viewers.

However, it must be said that marriages are symbolically formed in rural interior and tribal areas where girls get married even before they are mature enough to reproduce and are socially married at the time of the *gauna* of girl (*gauna* meaning sexually able to produce children or to be adequately fertile to reproduce). As such maternal mortality tends to be higher as reproduction takes place earlier when the female is not sufficiently mature both physiologically as well as maturationally. Such arranged marriages of the early maturing female has dire consequences in maternal and infant mortality, where such physiologically immature marriages take place and consummation occurs quickly the mother is anemic and often cannot hold up through the birth process and more often producing an anaemic, underweight and weakling progeny.

Thus, we find a variety of pre-marital heterosexual relations existing during the adolescent years. Such relations usually occur among high school adolescents where both sexes are in the same social and scholastic group. As they become older, the sexual attraction becomes stronger and they get involved in sexual relations, especially more frequently in the elite and rich upper classes where they practice contraception. This sociological and geoecological pattern shifts when we view heterosexual relations in the middle socio-economic class. In the latter, the parents are keen that the children should concentrate on their studies and become professionally oriented as they grow up to be adults. To this end, parents in this class are constantly positively reinforcing in terms of achievement and they tend to build up a higher need for achievement which then deflects the adolescent from career pathway. However, there is a conditionality in these situations. Where parents are busy working and where children are not in contact with their parents since both the parents are employed, communication and interaction becomes less and the parents are hardly aware of what their adolescents are doing while they are hard at work, building professional careers for themselves. Often times, this expectation does not come to fruition. Adolescents being non-supervised tend to slacken in their studies. Parents who depend upon expensive tutors to see that their children do their course work are often disappointed as many of the coaching classes are merely shops and are not very successful. For, while they might be in earnest about their children, the children may not meet parental expectations. If we turn from such an ecology to the vast rural ecology where children especially the female tend to drop out from school earlier than the male (*Ministry of Human Resources Development, Government of India, 2000-01)*, their acumen towards goal-attainment is very poor and many of them take to working at medium type technical and vocational jobs after an incomplete school education. That is if at all they complete a fair number of years of education. This is, of course, not a *carte blanche* statement. There might be genuine students who strive to get ahead in their studies, work hard and attain a good position. For example, there are several magnates across the world who have in their childhood lived in villages, but have achieved well through their own efforts.

On the other hand, there are scores of village migrants who move to urban areas and work hard to achieve professionally. Therefore, much depends upon the motivation and the need to achieve of the adolescent, whether urban, rural, migrant or living in originally high achievement-oriented families.

It is not unusual to find adolescents in a state of confusion about their future goals, as they are unable to live in a world that is achievement oriented. Often, parents are careless about the abilities of their children to study, work hard and achieve professionally. On the other hand, there are parents who work hard to see that their children do achieve and are often disappointed by the poor efforts of these very children. Therefore, much depends on the interactive abilities of parents and child. If affordable, these adolescents work part-time and learn to dress and imitate their counterparts they observe in movies and magazines. Therefore, throughout these scenarios, it is apparent that the motivation, the will to achieve and to become successful is mostly inherent in the adolescent himself or herself. At the same time, it seems that such adolescents are not deterred by heterosexual attractions which deviate them from their studies and professional goals.

Frequently those who are able to afford such modernized lifestyles, get along somehow. But there are those who have no access to money to afford what they want and so they tend to fall into disreputable ways like stealing, cheating and such like. In desperate cases such adolescents take to drug-taking, get hooked and eventually become drug addicts. Drug addiction, therefore, is a serious consequence of delinquency where drug addicts borrow or steal in order to have access to money to pay for their drugs. In a country as large as India where the education system and infrastructure is not stable, especially among the majority who are from the lower socio-economic classes, delinquency is a serious consequence arising from the confused behaviour and misconceptions about the identity that adolescents have. Male adolescents tend to run away from home, female adolescents tend to accept payment for the use of their bodies, become girl prostitutes, sell themselves into the hands of brokers just in order to keep their addictive habits going.

We will deal with interactional relations between the two generations in the next chapter. Here we will give a little anecdote about heterosexual behaviour.

> *Mohan and Ravi were walking along a wooded road and Ravi said to Mohan, "I hope at the next turn, we might discover a beautiful girl." Mohan jocularly said, "And, yet we might discover an ugly frog!".*

In an adolescent, there is no denying that there is a yearning, secretly or otherwise, to become a hero or a heroine in the eyes of those around him or her and to be admired. Whether an adolescent girl or boy is attractive or otherwise, there is a yearning or an eagerness to want to get from the world as much as possible. So, it was with Mohan and Ravi. This is a fairly common trend. In high school, boys and girls stay in their own groups and tend to poke fun at groups of the other sex, more so during recess time. It is not unusual for one boy to tell another like Mohan and Ravi, "arre yaar isn't Mala a beauty?", and unvaryingly the response would be, "yes, but she is proud and arrogant, whoever is ready to make a break-in with her, should also be ready to get a slap in the face." Adolescents at this stage are very sensitive as to their physical sexual selves with the other sex, and boys if daring, often make ploys to sidle up to the girls they admire and make innocuous comments. It is not different for Mohan and Ravi. They try to appear as much macho as possible. The less daring stand on the sidelines and watch enviously. Sometimes, getting to know a girl is like discovering a frog or a fish under an upturned stone. It is all a game of chance. If the boy and girl strike up a relationship, there is a gradual breaking away by the couple from the gang, male or female. As the adolescent grows older, we see more and more of such twosome couples forming. Sometimes, adolescents are eccentric in their choices, for some time they go along for a while with the girls of their choice and then suddenly drop them and string along with other girls. There is a break-away and a new heterosexual relation is formed. This is also true for Mohan and more especially Ravi. They delighted in making heterosexual friends and then dropping them whenever they felt like it. Such erratic behaviour is seen more frequently among males and often the boy is dubbed a Casanova. The girls are usually warned by their parents that such boys are turn-coats and the girls should stay away from them. But at times the adolescent girl may continue in her defiant behaviour because, as it is often said, these girls who fall into a pattern of hero-worship think they are madly in love and sometimes are unable to hold their physical, social and emotional behaviour in control. Boys, like Mohan and Ravi, on the other hand, are less emotionally rational. They see a girl and if she is admired and wanted as a friend by most of the boys in Ravi's gang, he does not think very much about who she is; her charm, her attractiveness and her sex appeal is all that matters to him just like Rani in Mohan and Ravi's school. Many times boys discover that the girls they latch on to turn out to be superficial and mainly interested in turning the heads of other boys, so as to make him jealous or she desires to be like a queenbee. Most girls are too shy and embarrassed to say outright that they try to prim themselves in order to attract the opposite sex like Shanthi in Rani's gang. But human nature is such that this is a natural attraction in adolescents to be enamoured by the opposite sex and to have a boyfriend is a big achievement. Exceptions of course occur. Boys are usually given a free rein and only get mild admonitions from their parents if they pay obvious attention to the opposite sex. Males are expected to appear virile and macho in their appearance and behaviour, while girls on the other hand are usually, especially in traditional homes, curbed by their mothers to appear inconspicuous and not brazen in their outward appearance. The same was true of Rani's and Shanthi's parents. But the natural urges propelled by the maturity of the physiological hormones attract them towards this kind of behaviour. It stands to reason that where adolescents remain relatively unsupervised and have a free hand in paying excessive attention to the opposite sex, they tend to appear confused and erratic. While Ravi was confident, Mohan was somewhat timid and follow the footsteps of Ravi often appearing by his side like a shadow. This is because several male adolescents are not sure of what they want and they keep changing their minds and, therefore, exhibit attention-seeking behaviour. There seems to be a natural tendency for such adolescents to behave in an imbalanced way concentrating on their physical appearance often to the detriment of developing their mental capacities. It is only when there is a balance between their attempts to look after both aspects simultaneously that there appears to be an equilibrium in their development. Where parents are too involved in their own egos and their own self-development, so there tends to be a lack of time given to their adolescent children or even to give them quality attention in terms of their studies and their personal problems. It is only when parents are discerning and take the time to interact with their adolescents in their difficult period of transition between childhood to adulthood that most of the problems of disharmony, misunderstanding and discord are discussed and clarified. Unfortunately, both Mohan and Ravi's parents are high professional achievers and tend to leave their sons to fend for themselves in their school work, only admonishing them to work harder now and again.

One might ask the question here: What should parents do to help their children in understanding themselves? The first and foremost is self-introspection by the parent himself or herself. How capable are they in advising and guiding their adolescent children? What kind of support, facilities exist in their environment and how can they utilize them to assist their adolescents? If, for example, Mohan and Ravi's parents interact more closely with their teachers, they might come to know more about their adolescents from the perspective of others. If they take the trouble to involve themselves from the primary school stage in the extra-curricular activities, in the neighbourhood, the school and other related institutions, they might be able to deflect their children to such needed and healthier activities and even at times encouraging them to take an interest in their outward appearances to the extent that mothers can advise their daughters and fathers their sons in a friendly camaraderie manner. This is especially true for young girls who go through a difficult period of menarchy than do boys who turn into manhood gradually with their problems of nocturnal emissions, stunted growth, and the embarrassment of their voice being cracked while speaking. These factors contribute to a sense of hesitancy, lack of confidence and in extreme cases, suffer from a lack of self-esteem and become introverted. Granted that some parents might find themselves unable to help their adolescents, but that does not mean that other avenues from the social support system are not available. It requires parental intuition and the will to help and not be indifferent. It is accepted that many things are better said than done. But parenting is not an easy task and certainly not with adolescents. Adolescents, on the other hand, try to break away from the parents' stranglehold and to be independent while searching for identity to find a niche in their social, peer group and support network. Even while boys seek the company of girls and the girls of boys in their group circles, the parents can help them to ease into these situations as naturally as possible and in a platonic manner. They can also help them separate their perceptions of the difference between what is genuine and what is not genuine. This is essential if adolescents are to achieve a sense of harmony in growing up, so that it helps the adolescent to be realistic about their heterosexual relationships.

Most importantly, adolescents have to be as wise as they can be at the stage of maturity to select friends who help them raise their personalities to a better level of competence, and it is not just any one of the friends who would serve the purpose anyhow. There has to be a compatibility and rapport between the adolescent and his selected friend or friends who help each other develop according to the norms of their given society.

A study indicated that adolescents who have to use coping mechanisms reported using problem-focus strategies in direct attempt made at understanding the problem and trying to resolve it, followed by the emotion regulating function behaviour (also referred to as wishful thinking). The coping behaviour infrequently reported was resorting to drugs, alcohol and sex (*Albuquerque, Z.M.; Rao, K.; Rao, S.; Subbakrishna, D.K.; and Prabhu, G.G., 1990)*.

In another study involving five nations (Hungary, India, Italy, Sweden and Yemen) it was found that, people of both genders in low and medium level provocative situations more often employ constructive and assimilative coping styles, whereas high anxiety provoking situations tend to mobilize avoidance (*Ola'h, A., 1995)*.

As is well-known, males have a strong ego and, therefore, exhibit greater adjustment to frustration, while girls, on the other hand, exhibit more frequently emotional reaction to frustrating situations (*Biswas, P.C., 1989)*.

Heterosexual relations in India are as varied as the different factors that impinge upon them such as geoecology, caste, religion and ethnicity. India being a large country with many sub-cultures, all these factors operate in different degrees. However, by and large, it is the fast-changing social and modernizing country and, therefore, difficult to predict its operations, whether smooth or otherwise in the area of heterosexual relations of adolescents.

REFERENCES

Albuquerque, Z.M.; Rao, K.; Rao, S.; Subbakrishna, D.K.; and Prabhu, G.G., 1990, "Coping Behaviour Among College Students", *Indian Journal of Clinical Psychology*, 17(1), 17-20.

Biswas, P. C., 1989, "Sex-differences in reactions to frustration among secondary school boys and girls", *Indian Journal of Applied Psychology*. 26(2), 6-8.

Foresta, C.; Bettella, A.; Ferlin, A.; Garolla, A.; Rossato, M. 1998, "Evidence for a stimulatory role of follicle stimulating hormone on the spermatogonial population in adult males. *Fertil Steril.* 69.

Jejeebhoy, S., 1998, "Adolescent Sexual and Reproductive Behaviour", *Social Science and Medicine*, 46 (10), 1275–1290.

Ministry of Human Resources Development, Government of India, *Selected Educational Statistics*, 2000-01.

Moreno, J.W., 1977, *Who Shall Survive?* Foundations of Sociometry: Group Therapy. Boston: Beacon House.

Ola'h, A., 1995, "Coping Strategies among Adolescents: A Cross Cultural Study", *Journal of Adolescence*, 18, 421-512.

Rana, J.P. Singh, 1998, *Marriage and Customs of Tribes of India*, MD Publications Pvt. Ltd., New Delhi.

Saraswathi, T. S., 1999, "Adult-Child Continuity in India: Is Adolescence a Myth or an Emerging Reality?", in T. S. Saraswathi (ed.), *Culture, Socialisation and Human Development: Theory Research and Applications in India*. pp. 211-216. New Delhi/Thousand Oaks/London: Sage Publications.

WHO, 2012, "Female Genital Mutilation", *WHO Factsheets*, at http:// www.who.int/mediacentre/ factsheets/fs241/en/, searched on 26. 12. 2012.

8

Educational Directions and Professional Goals

This chapter presents the scenario of the available education facilities, their utilization and the barriers that the adolescents meet in attempting to obtain a worthwhile education to meet their goals. However, after an education, what are the opportunities of utilization of such an education in terms of job opportunities and professional gains, which currently is a matter of great concern given the current day global recession, the main rider of which is lack of adequate job facilities and the non-availability of skilled personnel for them. We have detailed all through the previous chapters that the majority of adolescents either have little access to a completed education or that if they do the availability of jobs is very meagre for them.

Unfortunately, education for the young is generally understood to mean a high school education which is insufficient because in the main there is no one to one relationship between an education fitted for a particular job and the kind of education one gets. For this reason, many youngsters are disinterested in the completion of a high school education, because they do not have a focus on how it could be utilized in the future. True, there are some avenues in the vocational and technical fields, in training for jobs related to them as the training period is short and sometimes more profitable and timely for those who find it necessary to earn a livelihood after schooling. However, since the majority of adolescents come from impoverished families, even if they complete a high school education they usually tend to go into jobs such as casual jobs, often unpredictable in nature. We often find youngsters who say that they have to work in order to support themselves and their families of orientation since the amount of remuneration is related to the survival and upkeep of the families of orientation.

We give below the picture of the vast arena of adolescence who are the future generation of leadership. The following imagery will present the kind of scenario we are indicating:

> *It was the year 2025. Two astronauts sat in a space station belonging you know to which country. They were wearily looking ahead at nothing, almost nodding off to sleep. They were doing the same routine thing everyday for four months of the year, after which they spent six months at the nuclear facility. Suddenly, Jay woke up wide awake and stared down through his complicated stellarscope lenses, and jostled his friend Vijay, excitedly: "Look Vikay, look what's happening on our side of the Atlantic and Pacific". Vijay looked through his stellarscope lenses and said lazily: "Jay, after all these years, don't you recognize that this is a worldwide tsunami, and all those moving tiny objects you can see as little ants are people running up to higher grounds." "But, why are some running faster than the others?" "Don't you know anything about human nature, Jay. Look closer, the older ones are just stumbling along, the young ones are half-crawling and half walking, while the fastest runners are the youth. Why is it that? Each to his own, Dear Jay, the young are more self-motivated and physically agile, and when it comes to saving one's life, the "I" comes first. They are the future younger generation of leaders, remember and they will rule the world in the coming decades". "Yes", said Jay thoughtfully, "for, self comes first", and "Time is on the march", and "time belongs to the youth".*

Therefore, q.u.e.d. time is youth. "Is this true all over the world?" asked Jay. "You still haven't learnt that human nature, human physiogeny, human Phylogenesis, human orthogenesis, human genetic endowment are the same all over the world", said Vijay. "Is that so?" asked Jay, not understanding a word of what Vijay said. "Then, let's look at the countries other than ours". And they did. All over Africa, all over South East Asia, hordes of people, especially the young were moving to higher grounds to avoid the lashing waves. "There, there is the Indian subcontinent," pointing out to a place on the map, said Vijay, "and they are running for their lives", "Yes, of course… there are the hobbling old ones, the crawling little infants and the stalwart young ones," "Yes, I see", said Jay, "but the faster are the young ones." "I guess, they are the ones taking time by the forelock", said Jay. "Time and tide wait for no man and it is the youngsters who are the speediest, the cleverest and the most achievement-oriented", said Vijay. "Yes," said Jay "Time is on the side of the young, and time belongs to them".

Vijay, the inquisitive, continued to ask: "Are women equally spirited as men in the movement to the top? How are they distributed in that huge piece of land called India? Are there many very poor people? "How would I know", said Vijay.

They went to a statistical bureau and pored over the data, and what they came out with was an astonishing picture of statistics:

India has one-sixth of the world's population, it is the second highest populated country, has all religions, and about 2000 ethnic groups.

The major language is Hindi; however, English is also understood by many at least in smatterings.

The major rich States are Gujarat, Maharashtra, Punjab, Himachal Pradesh, Tamil Nadu, while the major poor States are Bihar, Orissa, Rajasthan and Uttar Pradesh.

India's population is estimated to be 1.8 billion, as of

2010. Two-thirds live in rural areas, and one-thirds of the total population are youngsters. How mentally and physically able are these youngsters to carry the future generation forward? About eleven per cent children aged 10-14 are employed in formal and informal enterprises, thus, losing out on the completion of a formal education. Only about two-thirds of these youngsters are in schools of some sort, many of them are of very poor calibre. What is sad is that a large proportion of female children who undertake the trouble to go to school at the cost of their daily home-making chores eventually fall back and do the household and domestic chores their grandparents have done before them. There is also inadequate infrastructure and quality of personnel. How many of them will become productive, and will have an opportunity to potentialize their skills? Currently, about eleven per cent of young adults do no work. More than 70 per cent children from the upper classes achieve well at school, while the lower social classes (Scheduled Castes and Scheduled Tribes) perform less ably. Dalits, Adivasis (Scheduled Tribe) and poor Muslims are far less likely to enrol in schools and more likely to drop-out sooner than others of the advantaged group. Therefore, they lack the necessary educational qualifications for seeking the facilities of a better life.

The major issue is, "To what extent is the young labour force likely to be competent in an era of increasing globalization and increasing world competition?" The answer depends upon how many people are likely to educate their children to be competent young professionals; how many are well-nutritioned and will live in a social context that is harmonious for personal well-being.

Given the increasing sophisticated technology the systems must be in place to warn them about nuclear explosions, tsunamis, rising tides and the increasing potential for man-made disasters; especially those related to ecology.

It follows logically that we have a major part of youth, about one-third and much more of females, who do not have professional skills, whether at the manual, paraprofessional or professional levels to be able to earn a decent living. The caveat is that opportunities are more advantageous for the rich elite, the nouveau riche and the growing upper middle class than for the majority of the poor. But the more serious question is that what happens to the drop-outs who then become the material for leadership in the future generation for which they do not have the necessary competence? We have only to compare people at the political level among themselves to note that many are poorly educated but yet have high-paying jobs, secured mainly through their ability of obtaining votes, for which many pay cash from black money sources.

What happens to the drop-outs, both male and female? What happens to the eleven per cent who do no work at all, and what happens to those scores of beggar children along the road-sides and at traffic stop-signs? This truncated proportion of the youths create a lopsided productivity group and the rest are unproductive including the young children and the elderly.

If these youths who have not reached the fullest potential of their educational capacity, and are doing jobs which do not challenge their potentials, then they might be frustrated and take to drugs and anti-social behaviour, given the opportunities out there "which are out of their reach during their youth" for it can be equivalent to the saying: "An idle mind is the devil's workshop."

What is the current estimate of the youths who work in desultory occupations which are not stable? There are no reliable data on these youths. Those in stable occupations among the young and the middle aged have to carry the burden of paying for the well-being of those who are not earning and, therefore, are unproductive. We know that the well-being of the unproductive poor, especially the females, in these poorer strata tend to be deplorable. Females marry early; have many children in quick succession and are depleted in health and nutrition statuses. Currently, maternal mortality is 300 per 100,000 and infant mortality is 60 per 1000 live births. Therefore, the efforts of the productive proportion become diluted when spread thinly for the upkeep of others less productive and yet have access to the same infrastructure facilities as do the minor productive proportion of the youth.

When we use the word youth, we mean both the sexes. But, unfortunately, the social and economic situation is not similar for both the sexes in India. Females are discounted even before they are born. Amniocentesis and female infanticide take their toll. Females in India are accounted as the second sex. Men will walk before, and women have to follow their footsteps. The result is a low female-male sex ratio, which will continue to be so until females are treated at par or nearly at par with males, especially in terms of physical and educational care.

If one were to examine these details little more closely, they are exacerbated by the demeaning phenomena of low castes. There are some who live by standing on the shoulders of others and these are the upper castes. India is ranked 124th in the Physical Quality of Life (PQL) index (United Nations, Human Development Report, 2002), which is an irony considering that its GDP is growing faster than ever before.

Thus, we see that the future picture about youngsters in India is pretty dismal. It is only the upper middle class and the upper classes who are probably better educated who bring up their children to be competent in line with comparative global standards. We are currently witnessing a large number of well-qualified youngsters who opt for jobs in other countries, especially of the West which, in spite of their having to struggle, manage to have a better quality of life. Now we understand that even in the West the youngsters who group up in places like America, Spain, Greece and Italy usually opt to work in better-paying jobs and curiously in the Middle East which is in a politically unstable situation.

> *Witness the many private gold star schools in major cities where fabulous sums are paid as entrance fees, whether the child so gaining entrance is competent or not.*
>
> *India is said to be an economically developing country. It is not known the position of India regarding social development as social development implies equality, fraternity and liberty. This does not seem to be so. In any village in America, one will find similar amenities from village to village. In Indian villages, the scattered few roadside eating places will only offer you* roti *and* dal. *These are only for the lucky people who have access to highways where these* dhabas *(eating shops) exist and there are many who do not have even marked roads to go from one village to another. Therefore, the plights of these economically disadvantaged, socially unknown deprived people who are relatively untouched by technology are unknown figures. The rich guzzle while the poor have little to guzzle on. We may arrive at guestimates, but we only have to look at the daily large streams of migrants of rural and tribal areas to cities and towns to guess what their plight is, in their place of origin. Such migrants live a daily survival life dependent upon manual work.*
>
> *It is not unusual to find scores and scores of such casual labour waiting along building construction sites hoping that the building contractors would hire them for work. Very few among them are the young. Where are these youngsters, who come from rural and tribal areas? They may be found in scores at railway stations, at market places, at bus-stops assisting petty cash-shop traders or even ganging themselves up into little Wall-marts carrying all kinds of items for trade at bus-stop and road signs along roads. It is said that "they also serve to stand and wait."*

The above general scenario set the stage for understanding adolescents in their different frames. For, there are always two sides to the story: while some labour, the others live off their labour. The fortunate few, who are mostly the rich usually achieve a college education, generally aspire to go abroad for further education and perhaps migrate. As the saying goes, a half-filled glass is still half empty. This migration of the youth, of course, is a familiar brain-drain phenomenon, but certainly it is not the dregs that are left behind. It is a simple fact that India as a country with a large poor population is unable to provide the necessary basic facilities for a satisfactory standard of living for all.

Therefore, a logical premise is that from the above scenario, we need to stress that adolescents in India, unlike in countries of the economically developed world, do not have homogeneous opportunities, do not have homogeneous facilities, and in actual fact are treated heterogeneously. Where the young are productive, the country usually prospers. If one were to write a book on all the adolescents in India, it would be a misnomer as adolescents live in different ecologies and have different facilities. Further still, there are grades of the caste system and there is an enormous number of different ethnic groups, sub-religious groups with varying economic standards. Since, the child is the product of his environment and knowing that the environment is poor, we can surmise that the average youth in India is short-changed of his necessities to become a well-developed personality.

Curiously with this lack of turn-out of educated school and college children, from the beginning of the Constitution education of primary school children was mandated, but as we can see the figures do not correspond with what is expected. This is in spite of the fact that compulsory primary school education has been reiterated from one Five Year Plan to another.

The Directive Principles of the States Policy of the Constitution of India obligate the Indian States to make provisions for free and compulsory primary school education for all children. However, for more than six decades after Independence, India has not been able to successfully implement this mandate by instituting adequate educational infrastructures and providing for trained personnel, competent enough to keep the interests of adolescents in schooling, the major obstacle being that most adolescents are from the poor social strata, who cannot complete a high school education, therefore, falling out of school with incomplete education as many of them have to earn a living in early adolescence.

Thus we can see that despite the mandates, discussions, conferences and seminars about the importance of primary school education for the young, the effort to institute structures, to train teachers and to have a good monitoring system deplete the implementation.

To rectify this situation, in 2009 the Government of India enacted the Right to Free and Compulsory Education for Children aged between 6 to 14. This includes high school education.

A report on the status of implementation of the Act was released by the Ministry of Human Resource Development on the one year anniversary of the Act. The report admits that 8.1 million children in the age group 6-14 remain outside the pale of schooling and there is a shortage of 508,000 teachers country-wide. Parallel reports by Non-Governmental Organisations point out that several legal commitments in the Act have not yet been implemented (*Summiya Yasmeen, 2010*).

Still fewer numbers of Indian adolescents attain higher education, as it is simply unaffordable in their given situation of constrains of whether to earn or to learn. It is apparent that the education pathway must lead somewhere to remuneration. It is now well-known that tribal and rural children do not have horizons that show them the skills by which this education could be used professionally. At the most the high school children of these outlying areas either come to urban areas for doing unskilled jobs or continue in their place of origin with whatever job opportunities are available, especially in the occupations of their forefathers, and mostly in agriculture. Further, staying in agricultural jobs under the changing situation, where the local market has to compete with imports from other countries, the average farmer finds it difficult to have a satisfactory income in relation to the growing Gross National Product. Further, the situation is complicated by the Government's attempt to introduce the Foreign Direct Investment schemes, as there is much protest that it would deplete the earnings of the small farmers and casual labourers.

Thus, such high schoolers not having appropriate channels to utilise their education professionally are often tempted to delinquent methods of obtaining money such as peddling of drugs, and the carrying back and forth for the middlemen such goods that are not legal (*Sen, Raj Kumar and A. Dasgupta*). These youngsters are often exploited for other purposes also such as acting on behalf of those who run whore houses. Unfortunately, many of these youngsters become drug addicts themselves *Dr. Nilima Mehta, 2008, Child Protection and Juvenile Justice System, for Children in need of care and protection. Published by Childline India Foundation, Bombay.*

Informal training in trading shops might offer skills that could provide poor paid jobs such as working as mechanics, repairers, assistance in shops and other manual labour that pay poorly and do not require much competence in the work that they do. So several youngsters in urban areas are found, according to the ILO, to be working at desultory and casual inconsistent jobs (*Mitra, Arup, 2008*). Otherwise, they tend to find casual labour in the outlying towns or, still worse, continue with the family occupation where they have learned skills informally within the family and, therefore, do not move out of the orbit of casual farming labour. If the adolescent brave the opportunity and moves to work in nearby towns and cities, he suffers from a feeling of *anomie*.

When delinquency in adolescents is apparent, they are put into Juvenile homes for rehabilitation. The Juvenile Justice Act instituted in 1986 provides for the identification and trials by Juvenile Justice Boards whereby children are put into state run juvenile care homes for the purposes of rehabilitation. After treatment if considered to be capable of returning to the society, their approbation officers monitor them. However, the care given in such homes needs to be carefully monitored for the adequacy of facilities and personnel, medical care and work that would be of utility on their return to the society (*Bakshi, P.M., 1993*).

When they return to society even though they are under probation, there is a probability that they continue to indulge in the previous delinquent habits. Therefore, it seems that many of these Homes do not prepare the delinquent juvenile for adequate efficiency on their return back to society.

There have been several small-scale studies on juvenile samples, mostly of males since females exhibit very few delinquencies that are noticeable to the public eyes.

One study, for instance, of a slum area indicated poor family supervision of the pre-adolescent and adolescent males who were either drop-outs or still were in primary schools and were indulging in thieving, forming gangs, using abusive language, teasing females and without any perceptible goals in sight (*Dassi, A., and Khan, M.Z., 2000*). A survey in Kolkatta measured delinquent attitudes on a sample of children. About 16 per cent indicated the risk of delinquent behaviour where there were high disregard for social values and high external locus oriented behaviour control. They displayed low anxiety tolerance (*Deb, S. "A study on the cognitive dispositions of school students of Calcutta conducive to delinquency", Indian Journal of Criminology, 21(2), 27-37*).

A study by Diaz, S.M. (1993) showed that recent social changes have affected the lifestyles of many youngsters. They are apt to be affected by social media and the growing wealth around them, when they themselves cannot keep up to the standards of well-being they observe in the rich. This condition incites them to delinquent behaviour. This study stresses community involvement in guidance and counselling. It is well-known that the infrastructure to cater to the needs of these youngsters is insufficient. Therefore, it seems necessary that the schools themselves, should from primary class onwards, provide guidance, counselling and try and involve parental and community participation in such activities so that the elderly parents can monitor the lifestyles of their adolescent children.

Another study on delinquents indicated that poor family relations and deprivation of care and love provoked youngsters to become delinquents (*Misra, S.S., 1977*).

These few selected studies indicate that delinquency does not occur due to inherent trait tendencies but that the environment propels them towards delinquency when there is no adequate bonding with the family in communication and guidance and also when there is no adequate bonding between the adolescence and his family network. Delinquency also arises when there is disturbance in the family and disorganization such as alcoholism and abuse. More especially it is likely to escalate when there is no guidance and counselling to direct the adolescent in the right direction. Internal factors can be frustration, a suffering of guilt and conflict between the adolescent, his peers and the family. In other words, for a smooth adolescent growth and development, it is essential that there is equilibrium between the adolescent and his environment, both human and material.

Such like studies suggest that the community, the school and the parents should be involved in monitoring their adolescents' educational performances and show an interest in these processes so that the adolescents might not deviate into anti-societal activities. However, it must be said that, most children are not inclined towards delinquency. It is only those who are poorly supervised and unmotivated who tend to fall into delinquent ways. It is usual to find that, in the upper class delinquency is not common as parents have sufficient wealth to put their children through schools of prestige where monitoring and guidance is adequately available.

At the same time it is essential to indicate that there is more a tendency for male adolescents to become delinquent than it is for female. Male adolescents have the freedom to move around, to mix with different peer group, to experiment with drugs and alcohol. Since they are relatively free to do so in these activities without adult guidance, there is a greater likelihood for these anti-tendencies to go unchecked outside the realm of the knowledge of parents and elders. Male adolescents do not expect their parents to monitor their behaviour in a strict manner. This can occur in any socio-economic class, high or low. Females, on the other hand, are over-protected and are usually monitored in their geographical movements. The parents tend to see that they are in the company of other females and are less likely to move around freely without being monitored.

Education in India, after high school, should be directed towards the goal aspirations of youngsters who are keen on studies and keen on using their studies for future professional development (*Anil Bordia, 2009*). This is noticeable among the middle class groups who are striving to imitate the upper class and who are attempting to lead better lifestyles. This class is inclined to a large extent to encourage their children to work hard to attain good grades and become "somebody". Parents of middle class children work sufficiently hard to provide their youngsters with tutorial classes and other necessities so that the youngsters are motivated to obtain high levels of education. It is well-known that high school scores are important markers to enter into university education.

Although female participation in education has increased steadily after Independence, it is still below 50 per cent at all stages of education as can be seen from the following figures:

Year	*Primary (I-V)*	*Upper Primary (VI-VIII)*	*Secondary/Sr. Secondary/ Intermediate (IX-XII)*	*Higher education (Graduation and above)*
(1)	(2)	(3)	(4)	(5)
1950-51	28.1	16.1	13.3	10.0
1960-61	32.6	23.9	20.5	16.0
1970-71	37.4	29.3	25.0	20.0
1980-81	38.6	32.9	29.6	23.2

(*Contd.*)

(*Contd.*)

(1)	(2)	(3)	(4)	(5)
1990-91	41.5	36.7	32.9	33.3
1999-00	43.6	40.4	38.9	38.7
2000-01*	43.7	40.9	38.6	39.4
2004-05*	46.7	44.4	41.5	38.9

*Provisional.

Source: Sandhya Rani, G., "Women's Education in India—An Analysis", *Asia-Pacific Journal of Social Sciences*, Vol. III (1), January-June, 2010, pp. 106-124.

The reason for this slow increase in school education for female is because of the preponderance of traditional socio-religious norms where females are more protected than the males (*Kantikar, S.D. 1996*).

It is the thinking among scholars and intellectuals that if India is to become a developed country, it requires to fill the gaps mainly in the education sector and also in the understanding and practice of honest ethical behaviour by the people as education alone is insufficient to bring about development. In this era of social change, it is the modern thinking in the country that females should be just as well educated as the males. Many barriers existing in the country to educating female children are difficult to erase since they are part of the social values in the socialisation process (*Dube, L., 1988*). The parental generation is more keen that the female child is educated in homely ways and is well-prepared for a married family life (*Sudha, B.G., and L.V. Tirth, 1986*).

The tendency to exclude interaction between females and males in the Indian society, even on a platonic basis, is another barrier in the exclusion of the females in rural areas from higher education. On the other hand, given the dynamic social changes that affect urban living, females are encouraged to utilize opportunities for entering into professional education. There are many young women today who are studying for their MBA and even study online to improve their educational abilities to obtain professionally lucrative jobs, especially in the corporate world.

When there is an artificial barrier, there is a tendency to increase the duality between males and females, where females are considered to be exclusive of male interaction. In fact, educational institutions which have both sexes have a healthier environment and create easy relationships which are friendship-based between the sexes. Exclusion, in fact, sometimes tends to heighten the secretive interaction of male and female adolescents outside the family and social networks.

Gender-inclusive teaching will help to utilize the 50 per cent female resources meaningfully to a larger extent than currently being utilised. Females are very agile at being teachers in primary and secondary schools, besides becoming nurses and technicians in entrepreneurial activities like shop-keeping, salesgirls and such like. This would also help in women's empowerment. Presently, the majority of girls do not have access to quality education, which undermines the overall efficiency of female human resources as almost 50 per cent do not get even a completed primary-school education. Conservatism, old values, superstitions and traditions widen the gap between India and developed countries in modernized behaviour. Further, with differences increasing between the rich and the poor in the country itself, it tends to widen the gap between the educated rich and the uneducated poor. This has been a trend over the past years.

In the decades to come, as greater numbers of adolescents seek institutions of higher education, it will need a huge requirement of infrastructure and a larger number of trained personnel. Currently, the majority of primary schools are of poor quality with indifferent staff and since monitoring is poor many a time classes are not taken and teachers do not appear. One would assume that with the programme of community development, rural employment guarantee scheme and many such smaller schemes several of them being assisted by NGOs it may be assumed that more females are in school. However, the barrier of traditional restraint continues to operate in spite of the best intentions of even these small-scale NGOs (*Mehrotra, Deepti Priya, 2006).*

If teaching is modernized as per the requirements of the day, India will be in high competition with other developing countries and, therefore, could have a better possibility of creating competitive professionalism. The real reasons behind the present lack of these are social and economic lacunae. There is also lack of enthusiasm and commitment on the part of the polity who are engrossed in many scams and self-aggrandizement. The leaders in the polity only speak in words and not in these actions.

Societal norms indicate that given the patriarchal system of Indian societal structure, males are the first to avail of education facilities as they are the bread-winners of the family. Society mandates that females should take care of their children and their homes, and so education for them lags behind as they have little time for pursuing education and, therefore, in most of the poorer sections, who constitute about 65 to 70 per cent of the population, there is little opportunity for improvement of skills for the rural female. Agricultural women in fact spend about 14 hours of their routine in the care of the home, children and attending to agricultural tasks (*Jennie Dey, 1984*). The net result is females continue to work at low paying jobs whether family oriented or in family occupations. Their economic activities in agriculture and other family occupations and chores are not taken into account as their contributions to the economy of the family or of the country. The females in social reality are perceived as the receivers of the occupational gains of men so as to take care of their children and their household chores.

A further barrier is that merit is not the only reason for gaining entrance into higher educational institutions. The reservation quota is also a caveat in playing down merit in accordance with providing for those who are the disadvantaged section of the populations many of whom because of their poverty status also tend to withdraw their female children from the schooling system.

College education is not taken full advantage of as it is not free and it is difficult for the poor enthusiastic students, both males and females, to enter into college and have completed college education because the next question is where can these college educated adolescents obtain matching jobs. The Government has tried for the last six decades to help enroll both male and female children in primary school so that they would be motivated to go on to secondary school and even if they do not go to college, they could be employed in small-scale routine jobs where they can use at least the knowledge that the high school gives them. There are numerous obstacles faced by the disadvantaged social groups like Scheduled Castes, Scheduled Tribes, poor religious minorities and females in remote areas who have to travel long distances to school and back and, therefore, depletes their time for essential survival tasks in their daily routine. It is perhaps the main reason why they lose the opportunity for higher education.

Education is a significant torch-bearer for development. If there are no adequate free channels for education beyond primary school into high school and into technical and vocational job opportunities, the adolescents will be shortchanged in terms of professional skills.

If female children are less likely to complete high school education, why is it that male children who have more chance of completing education do not do so? For them the choice is between earning an income, however casual the jobs available, and the requirement of completing an education which requires money. They do not have the resources to undergo training in technical and mechanical jobs which could give them a pathway into the utilisation of their education and training for profit. Even if they complete a high school education, they may not have the facility to set up technical shops. One would suppose that given a free education all the way and a stipend, to help them in their education, this might perhaps be a telling incentive for getting professional education and job. Free education up to 14 years as stipulated in the current Right to Education Act does not lead them into jobs that are available and which pay them remuneration however small. In sum, one might say,

(a) It is not that adolescent do not want to be educated and to increase their knowledge;
(b) That this increased knowledge can give them access to well-paid jobs; and
(c) Their concerns are for here and now to support families.

The rich have little problems in planning out goals for their children's profession and those who are very rich even send their children abroad for training in professional skills like doctors, engineers and IT professionals. The middle class parents have to sacrifice in order to urge their male adolescent children work hard towards a profession. In many cases the children are reinforced by their parents to be goal-achievement oriented. This is difficult in view of the fact that many times parents themselves are illiterate and occupied with earning a survival income. In many middle class families parents are apt to say we want our children to be better than when we ourselves were children and where we did not have these kinds of opportunities. In the middle class, adolescent females are urged to study towards a profession, for the feeling is now that an education which is professionally oriented will help them during the time they have to look after their own family where other consequences might occur such as divorces, separations and low earning of the husband.

Thus, we see that while education up to primary education and now under the RTE Act up to 14 years is free and compulsory, the poverty environment of the majority presents barriers to the attainment of an education that provides an opportunity for well-paid jobs.

Thus it is seen that among the middle and upper classes the involvement of parents in the education of their adolescent children is significantly important. However, this does not appear to be the picture in the Indian scenario. Below is a little anecdote about such instances.

> *Mrs. Athwal was getting very flustered. Everyday she had to face this group of unruly 16-17 years old and try to teach them to be serious about their studies. She knew and dreaded the hammering she would get from parents at PTA meetings. They always asked her how their individual child was doing. She was quite sure they never ask the individual child himself.*
>
> *To most parents in India, schools are treated as strange institutions out there. They tend to think that getting their children ready for schools, and depositing them safely in the school premises or seeing that he is safely transported back and forth and keeping him well-dressed when they send him to school, finishes their task unless of course they are told by the teacher, the child is doing poorly in his grades and they wipe off their hands in this case also by engaging tutors even if they can ill-afford them and even if either or both, namely the husband or wife, are capable of tutoring their own children.*
>
> *Amongst the middle and the upper classes, getting their child admitted to a school, where grades are reported to be high amongst children so that they can tell their friends that their children are in good school seems to be as far as parents are willing to go in terms of their adolescent children's education. Few parents take the trouble to read the course work, the time-table and other class-room activities of their child and they are little interested in how the character of their child is shaping under the guidance of the school and a particular teacher who happens to teach their child. Teachers like Mrs. Sabbarwal are nineteen to the dozen. They come to their occupation with their own problems, with less preparation than they should have and what is worse, is that there is little attention to what they teach routinely in a*

similar fashion every year. It is enough for the parents to look at the report cards and from that to infer that the child is not doing well because the teacher is not good, the teacher harasses their child, the teacher is indifferent in evaluating their child's performance and, by and large, treats the child as another statistic in the huge class rooms to which most teachers are subject to.

The misnomer that a school is good simply because it is high-fee charging does not end the story. There is no parent involvement in assessing the quality of the school because by and large parents themselves are ignorant of these fine lines of criteria of assessment, whereas in the west there is much literature on the types of schools that are available on the internet from which educated parents might be able to assess the comparative quality of different schools and select the best for their child. However, on the other hand, since there is a high growth rate of adolescents, in respect of availability of facilities, most children end up studying in State schools which are free, but suffer from lack of teacher interest, parental involvement and school monitoring. In most schools, because of the growth of population there is a rush for admissions and often parents have to resort to what is euphemistically called the "entrance fee", with the result that bright and intelligent children do not get into good high schools because their parents cannot afford the high entrance fees (donations).

Any one child is not like any other. Each is an individual with different ways of reacting to what is taught, especially if they are at different levels of intelligence. To treat all children in a class room as belonging to one homogeneous group is psychologically untenable as each one has a unique differential intellectual ability with differing IQ levels and differential goal-oriented perspectives. A teacher's ability to treat each child separately as a unique individual is often beyond her comprehension or if she does have the comprehension, the contents are beyond her frame of reference.

Children in India are over-burdened with the quantity of information which is fed down to them like force-feeding a patient through a tube, whether they understand it or not the information is inevitably to be ingested as it is expected to be completed within a certain time and, therefore, rote learning of topics is a favourite methodology used by most teachers. There is little attempt to instil creativity to develop the child's own cognitive abilities which is a more sure way of the child's understanding of what is being taught. We are not unfamiliar with the fact that many small book shops sell guidebooks for assisting students at examinations. Children who have not applied themselves to their studies turn gratefully to these guide books for these guide books are skilfully oriented towards the curriculum from which teachers use their data for setting up the examination questions. It is no small wonder that often children "mug up" the answers to such questions just before the exams, to spew it out if they are fortunate to have the same questions asked and promptly forget what they have learnt to repeat by memory. Therefore, it is often not a teacher's fault who has to complete a huge amount of course work in as short a time as possible through artfully delegating to the child his homework (to find his own answers). Children are often loaded with homework and in despair parents often "help them" do their homework, so what eventually appears on the teacher's table as the child's homework is really the material doctored by parents and tutors. The student is usually lulled into thinking that he has learned his work successfully and the parents revels in the "child's accomplishment", all living in an illusionary world. For this reason, quantity teaching does not lead to qualitative learning. Most children, who have an inherent eagerness to learn, to locate other sources of information related to the topics, on the internet, to ask more questions and elicit more answers from the teachers indicates an

> *intelligent child, which is not a phenomenon which appears often. A passive imbibing child who accepts information without question has not learned much and, therefore, his potential has not been fully empowered.*

The education of the adolescent is also fraught with problems since the adolescent has many other interests and, therefore, the quality and proficiency of the teaching should be challenging enough to reinforce the adolescent to move forward towards an educational goal. If infrastructures are poor, if teachers are poorly trained, the system of teaching because of the numerous numbers of State schools tends to fall into a poor quality teaching which is unchallenging and uninterested. However, in the middle income groups, there seems to be much interest taken by the parents to involve themselves in the adolescent's education since they know that the adolescent is sensitive and, therefore, keep the child focused on accumulating progressive knowledge.

REFERENCE

Anil Bordia, (2009), Education for All – Mid Decade Assessment", *Education of Youth and Adolescents in India*, National University of Educational Planning and Administration.

Bakshi, P.M., (1993), *"Juvenile Justice Boards", Indian Journal of Criminology*, 21 (1), pp. 15-26.

Dassi, A., and Khan, M.Z., (2000), "Family and the emergence of deviant behaviour among children and adolescents", *The Indian Journal of Social Work*, 61 (3), pp. 420-434.

Deb, S. "A study on the cognitive dispositions of school children of calcutta conducive to delinquency, *Indian Journal of Criminology*, 21(2) 27-37.

Diaz, S.M. (1993), "Community education for combating juvenile delinquency", *Indian Journal of Criminology*, 21 (2), 1-10

Dube, L., (1988), 'On the construction of gender: Hindu girls in Patrilineal India', in K. Chanana (ed.), *Socialisation, Education and Women*. pp. 166-192. New Delhi: Orient Longman.

Jennie Dey, *Women in Rice Farming Systems* (focus: sub-Saharan Africa. Food and Agricultural Organisation of the United Nations, Rome, 1984).

Kantikar, S.D. (1996), "Gender Discrimination in the Family: Views and Experiences of Teenage Girls", *The Journal of Family Welfare*, 42 (4), 32-38.

Misra, S.S., (1977), "Juvenile Delinquency and Parental Deprivations", *Indian Journal of Clinical Psychology*, 4(1), pp. 69-73.

Mehrotra, Deepti Priya, (2006), 'Impact of Gender Discrimination on Girls in School in Four States of India', New Delhi: *Plan Internationl.*

Mehta, Nilima, (2008), *Child Protection and Juvenile Justice System for Children in Need and Protection*, Bombay : Childline India.

Mitra, Arup, (2008), *The Indian Labour Market: An Overview. ILO Asia-Pacific Series, Sub-regional Office for South Asia*, New Delhi.

Omvedt, G., and V. Geetha, (2006), *Patriarchy*, Lancaster, U.K.: Gazelle Book Services Ltd.

Sen, Raj Kumar and A. Dasgupta, (eds.), (2003). *Child Labour in India.* New Delhi: Deep & Deep.

Sudha, B.G., and L.V. Tirth, (1986), "Effects of Parental Careers and Marriage Expectations on the Problems of Rural and Adolescent Girls in Relation to their Religion and Socio-Economic Status", *Indian Psychological Review*, 30(3): 9-17;

Summiya Yasmeen, (2010), RTE Act: "First Anniversary Report", *Educationworld Online*, 7-5-2010, retrieved 4.2.2013.

United Nations Human Development Report, 2002.

9

Traditionality and Modernity

The world of today for the adolescent is not the same as it was when he was a pre-school child. The inter-linkages between country and country, especially between the developing and the developed, are growing very fast. India is a member of many international organizations besides the UN and its branches and rightly so since these international organisations, especially UNICEF, UNFPA and the ILO are concerned with the problems of adolescents in poor countries. The UNFPA has indicated much interest in the lives of adolescents, more so because of the growing promiscuity between the two sexes. The probability is that greater promiscuity impels greater risk for aids and pre-marital sex. The growing interest in inter-sex relations has been spurred on by the encouragement in watching other countries through the social media and through other forms of interaction between the sexes. However, it must be said that there is a difference between the upper and lower classes in India in heterosexual relations. The lower class adolescents, which form the majority, are less exposed to Western cultural influences as their lives are more sheltered and farther removed from attractive influences that promote promiscuity than the upper class adolescents. The imitation of the West by upper class adolescents are promoted mainly by their possession of a great deal of pocket money given to them without questioning by the elders and availability of mobiles, movies and chit-chat over the internet. This entices them to watching porno movies, pub-drinking, going around malls, going off together on jaunts without much adult supervision, staying out late and paying less attention to studies and the goals of attaining professional jobs. This phenomenon is a growing area of conflict between the older and the younger generation. Much of this freedom of interaction is because the society itself is also absorbed in making money.

Parents think that by earning more money they can offer a better lifestyle for their children. They let their children go out on their own, do not check which groups they are after or which haunts attract them whereby they can buy all kinds of drugs and, therefore, confuse their own identity. With the growth in economy, parents who could not earlier earn much are now able to give their children more money. The way the money is spent is no longer a matter of concern to these parents as they themselves have no time to supervise their children's activities.

Appadurai (1990) has delineated five possible scenarios that have affected the Indians in the globalised world. These are:

(1) *Ethno-scapes*: People who move between nations, such as tourists, immigrants, exiles, guest-workers, and refugees;
(2) *Techno-scapes*: Technology often linked to multinational corporations;
(3) *Finance-scapes*: Global capital, currency markets, stock exchanges;
(4) *Media-scapes*: Electronic and new media; and
(5) *Ideo-scapes*: Official state ideologies and counter-ideologies.

These factors will naturally affect the growing adolescents, but, as said before, they affect mainly the upper echelons of society. The ones from the middle class will strive towards imitating the technocratic groups, but will almost always face frustration since they do not have the monetary means to rise to the imitated statuses. The poorest of the poor who live in tribal and far-flung rural areas will hardly be touched by modernisation and will continue to live the way they had lived for generations. This is of course with a little exception that they gain from being in touch with the modernized urban world around them. Under such circumstances, with the diversion of youth to other than educational skills, adolescents will be far removed from modernized ventures. Further, it is well-known that the ethos of honesty in the given scenario of political corruption is much less than it should be in order to provide youth with jobs that they truly deserve by their own efforts. Much is done through "*sipharish*" (nepotism). It is not unusual to hear or know of parents seeking good paying jobs from the polity or the bureaucrat in their vicinity. The future generation have to look forward to a life of great struggle and without the necessary skills, it will be a hard task to raise the country forward. There will continue to be depletions made by black money deposited in foreign banks which is the privileges of the polity. Instead of being used for the development skills of the youngsters, they are hidden to retain their own ego-driven positions in the politics of the land. Thus, the striving middle class knows that it cannot achieve high positions righteously and transparently. Therefore, facing them is a lifestyle that is shrinking in its economy and its ability to provide them with the wherewithal to increase their status. Therefore, the growing adolescent in the middle classes will be short-changed in their ability to live a satisfactory standard of life. Thus, while modernisation in the abstract implies better facilities, greater technology, and more innovation, at the same time the geo-ecology is also faced with shrinking resources and difficulties in obtaining suitable jobs without resorting to bribery and dishonesty. The ethos that existed before of deference towards the elders, of righteousness and of going through life transparently and honestly will all be pot-boiling. It is when the country wakes up and does justice to the majority of the poor that some kind of rise in standards may be expected. The adolescent generation who will be the future leaders of tomorrow will have much anguish to face in this scenario of bribe-taking and giving of non-transparent and non-accountable wealth done by elders and will leave them a legacy of having to struggle to survive.

The following story illustrates in some respect the lives of those who live and struggle strenuously in high-paying jobs and at high levels of positions where they travel from one country to another in their strenuous work:

As Jagdish's father got out of the plane on to the sleeve of the airport where the aircraft stopped, the attendants greeted him with a polite "goodbye, hope you had a comfortable journey". "Yes, thank you," he said, "I hope you had an easy time". "We did, thank you", said one little mischievous airhostess. But many of your co-passengers had a hard time resting. "Why," he asked. Cheekily the little airhostess said, "why, sir, you slept all through so noisily", Jagdish clasped his forehead in consternation. "Oh, my God," he said, "was I snoring so loudly all that time". They just smiled politely.

Jagdish couldn't blame himself. He was literally sleep-deprived being most of the time either flying to or from places or attending high-pressured meetings or attending to conference calls.

Globalization did take a toll of one's increasingly pressured lifestyle. He wondered what it would be like when his son's generation came to this stage. How his son would be groomed for this globalised living.

An example is that of Sheila and Meera. Sheila and Meera are staunch friends. In one incident, they were going to a school party held at the end of the year. Meera said, "My mother is so old-fashioned. She is always interfering with what I should wear, the make-up I should not use and how I should be meek and feminine", and yet, after the school party is over, I know that a group of boys and girls will go pub-drinking, DJ-dancing and yet when they come home, the girls will behave like feminine good girls and the boys could not be better as well-behaved young men, "Hah!" Meera continued: "It is a very difficult situation, I have to be careful all the time."

Sheila said in a pacifying tone, "you've got to play your cards well. You must know when to behave like a traditional well-brought up little girl and when you can be free to be as experimental as you want. Look at the TV channels, they are excellent models for behaviour. "Yes, *yaar*", said Meera. "It's such a bore, when to behave traditionally and when one can ape one's models."

In a free-wheeling and free dealing society such as the elite society in which circles Jagdish moved and in which circle Meera was on the other side of the fence, living the old fashioned traditional ways that her parents have imbibed in her, show the two parallel worlds betwixed and between modernity and traditionality.

The situation may be different when we talk about the upper classes and the lower classes. The upper classes take these social and technological changes in an easy fashion. The lower classes do not. While many parents in the lower classes are now striving to behave like the middle classes, working hard to send their children to schools to finish their education so that they could be better placed than them as adults. The children of the poor, on the other hand, are left to watch, to desire and to be frustrated while sitting on the opposite side of the fence, watching the rich in their gleaming cars, their "hep" clothes, their ostentatious ways of living, almost to the point of surfeit, while they themselves struggle with the scraps their parents bring home. There is naturally a huge resentment that builds up between the poor and the rich. On a small scale it is what Meera in our previous story experiences, hemmed in by a traditional family environment while she watches her other peers like Sheela having a free and leisurely modernized way of living.

What may we attribute these differences to? It is certainly the clash of ideologies. The rich have too much and the poor have too little and yet they live in the same environment. The lower class messenger boy sweats his way from bus to bus, to get to his office, before his boss, while his boss has a leisurely breakfast, a leisurely ride in a car and can appear any time he wants in the office. In a way life deals cards differently to different people. *Some are born great, some have greatness thrust upon them and yet many have to strive towards it.* The unfortunate part is that unlike in the olden days where the rich deliberately segregated themselves from the poor, lived in far away mansions in urbanized areas; the poor lived in ramshackle hamlets in them impoverished environs. Globalization, modernisation, increasing technology and sophisticated ways of living are what they perceive in others but cannot acquire for themselves. As such a disharmony prevails between the rich and the poor.

In the Western world, this difference is not so glaring. All people live in a fairly homogeneous fashion whether in congested metropolitan areas like New York, or in quite towns as in New Jersey which are States next door to each other, and have the same access to the same facilities. There are hardly any homes in the middle classes that do not have the usual fittings such as dish washers, washing machines, dryers, air conditioning and a couple of cars in the driveway. This is a far cry from India where many poor village and tribal people have to struggle hard just to survive, yet creeping into these villages are such modernized equipments, marketed by the relentless national and multinational corporations, such as mobiles, televisions, and such like. The only difference is that the poor can only see but not possess, but the rich cannot only see, but also possess such fascinating items ten times over.

Given the fast pace of globalization, there is a tendency for morals to be eroded and for crime and other anti-social behaviour to increase, often spurred on by unfair political clout, which in a sense also increases anti-social behaviour among the young *(Singh, S.N., 1997)*.

In other words, where technological development is uneven, social change lags behind for those who cannot benefit from it. Those in the middle classes can only encourage their children to work hard towards obtaining as much as they can and to attain a better life. Yet, it is important that a civic sense of ethics be inculcated in the total society, so that the rich respect the poor and their needs and follow a civic code just as much as it is imposed upon the poor. Unfortunately, we see stray cases where the rich can literally get away with murder so long as they have the political backing and monetary wealth, while the poor are punished for the slightest transgression and until and unless liberalisation affects most of the families which are poor, the poor get short-changed by lack of opportunity.

The Indian lives in two words: one of traditionality and the other of modernity. He also comes from differing ecologies. The traditional youth come from poor ecologies, while the rich living in urban areas come from well-to-do ecologies. However, much the poor might strive to compete with the rich they often lag behind, and their identity as an Indian becomes confused between whether he can live the life of a rich friend or have to struggle in the poor mire. These two kinds of youth live side by side, one envying the other and the envied flaunting his riches. Unlike other countries the distance between the rich and poor is far and wide. It will take eons for the poor to catch up with the rich, and for the traditional to become modernized.

It is easier for the rich to adopt and adapt the new ways of the West than it is for the poor to imitate the rich in India. No matter what is said and done, children who are socialized in a poor habitat, continue to lack the fineness of gracious living which is so easily available to the rich. For many the grass will always be greener on the other side of the fence. Traditions will continue in a tottering form for generations to come and homogeneity will take a long time in appearance on the stage in India.

It is important that at this juncture in the twentyfirst century we look at India from a futuristic point of view since the adolescents of today will be the adults of tomorrow and, therefore, the scenario should be looked at proactivity. Demographically, there will be a larger number of dependents on these future youth who will be at the helm of affairs in most enterprises in India in the future to come. Therefore, demographically, the burden on them of young children and the elderly will be heavy, since longevity is increasing, and the birth of children in the lower income groups is continuing unabated. The elderly are being kept alive through modern medicines and young babies are being produced in quick succession simply because the scheme of birth control amongst the poor has not been acceptable. A larger number of children for these poor households are because of an expectation that more children implies more security in their old age. Not only will this demographic factor change, but the socio-economic situation will differ from one decade to another. Social groups will be moving constantly and geographically across the States and also out of the country. Economically, the middle class is trying to climb the step of successful well-being with the knowledge that this can be done through better educational facilities and better job opportunities for which the skills are essential by education and appropriate training. The poor who are ignorant of this information of improved technology will suffer from information gaps and will be circumscribed by the little milieus in which they live. What then are the possibilities the adolescents of today can expect in terms of the future? As is well-known there is more heterogeneity and a large number of mini societies in India that can be counted for. Each little community subscribes to its own social norms and socio-religious beliefs. In spite of this heterogeneity and differential patterns of living, one concept stands out firmly. The Indian is deeply rooted in his religious rituals, in his belief in the scriptures, and in the existence of the *atma* and the *jiva* (*Bon Maharaj, Swami B.H., 1963).* These beliefs are also tied with the differences in caste where unfortunately at the same time the higher castes are the richer and the lower castes are poorer. This divide might to some extent close within the coming decades but because of the need of socio-religious rituals during births, marriages and deaths and other rituals of the lifecycle according to the Hindu norms there will always be a strong belief and practice in these domains.

An individual might be modernized in his outlook, in his behaviour, in society but within the privacy of his household and family, he is still religiously oriented.

What then is the outlook for the adolescent who lives in substantially lower strata?

The poor and the middle class, as is true of human nature, will always strive to move upwards.

Homogeneity is ensconced in religion, but heterogeneity is diverse in social-economic, demographic and related spheres. Therefore, describing behaviour, thought and belief in adolescence is not uniform. The differences will continue to play an important part in the adolescent and the adolescent's family trying to achieve a better standard of living for the adolescents. Given the wide scope of globalization where each country freely interacts with the other, there are likely to be dynamic changes throughout their life styles.

There are several definitions of modernity. Some are culture-specific and there are several core values. Modernity is related to the spirit of freedom, to question and to seek greater meaning of creativity. Modernity by itself is an abstract term, but implies a continuous process of enquiry of innovativeness, of creativity, of exploration and freedom from orthodoxy.

Modernity opens up the world and increases vertical and horizontal mobility. Change is the spirit of modernity. One is exposed to the plurality of different sets of human beings and their behaviour (*Berger, Peter L.; Berger, Brigitte; and Kellner, Hansfried, 1979)*.

Modernity implies the process of individuation. It is a radical shift from fatalism to active agency, from ascription to achievement, from positivity to meaningful choice (*Pathak, A., 2011, p. 16)*. Because of this freedom to experiment, to express, to innovate, rationalism becomes important in the advancement and progress of innovativeness.

India has a social historicity of being a traditional society. Until recently, modernity had not touched its surface as it was under the rein of feudal kings and the colonialists and so it had to find its own pathways, with little freedom to try out new themes of life. Perhaps, retaining these ancient parameters kept its circumscribed to its age-long secure ways against hoarding forces.

It stayed close to its traditional beliefs, as to the relationship between man and nature. Superstitions and ritual performances have kept it within these parameters. Over time, with the invasion of forces from the north, from the West and from sea trading countries, India became a mixture of many races. The Moghuls from the north-west, the British from the west and sea-traders from the African coast formed the conglomeration of mixed races. Therefore, one could find a Kashmiri adolescent, a Tamilian adolescent, a Gujarati adolescent and a Bengali adolescent all subscribing to being Indians; heterogeneity within a homogeneous nationality.

Yet, when we closely examine the lifestyles of these various heterogeneous individuals, they each have their own specific styles of living although they profess one culture. Heterogeneity is composed of many ethnicities, languages, regionalities and, more especially, sub-cultures, and yet while maintaining their own paradigms, they are expressly Indians.

As such, infancy, later childhood, adolescence, youth-hood and old-age have their own markers within this heterogeneity of age-differential lifestyles. There are some tribes which celebrate adolescence differently from others, and we find that there are various markers to define adolescence since in different sub-cultures there is no definable calendaring stages to mark adolescence and age is relatively unknown in most of the traditional rural, tribal, coastal, hill groups. They use religious events as chronological markers, for instance, the adherence to *samskaras*[1] in the "Hindu" paradigm. According to the *samskaras*, the stage of young adolescence is called the *brahmacharya* stage during which time the adolescent has to keep his celibacy and devote his entire time to learning the scriptures (*Singh, Y., 1977; Bhattacharya, N.N., 1996)*.

NOTE

1. The *samsakaras*, the four-fold stages called *ashramas* in the life of a Hindu, are very much akin to the categories of the stage of man in Ericksonian theory. The four *ashramas* are ***brahmacharya***, ***grihastha***, ***vanaprastha*** and *sanyas*.

REFERENCES

Appadurai, A. (1990), "Disjuncture and Differences in the Global Cultural Economy", in M. Featherstone (ed.); *Global Culture;* London: Sage. pp. 295-310.

Bon Maharaj, Swami B.H., 1963, *Jiva, Atma or Finite Self.* Vrindavan: Institute of Oriental Philosophy.

Berger, Peter L. Berger, Brigitte and Kellner, Hansfried, 1979. *The Homeless Mind.* New York: Penguin Books.

Bhattacharya, N.N., 1996, "Rites of Passage", in N.N. Bhattacharya (ed.), *Ancient Indian Rituals and Their Social Contexts,* Vol. XXIII (2nd revised and enlarged edition). Delhi: Manohar.

Pathak, A., 2011, *Modernity: Globalization and Identity.* Aakar Books. New Delhi.

Singh, S.N., 1997, "Youth in Urban Slums". Paper presented at the National Symposium on Youth in Urban Areas, organised at Institute for Development and Communication. Chandigarh.

Singh, Y., 1977, "Orthogenetic Changes in Cultural Traditions and Modernisation", in Y. Singh (ed.), *Modernisation of Indian Tradition (A Systemic Study of Social Change).* Faridabad, India: Thomson Press.

10

The Makings of Identity

In the foregoing chapters, an attempt has been made to intertwine several aspects of the growing personality. These are in the areas of psychological, social and physiological development during adolescence. Adolescence has been called the twilight zone since it is mainly a transitional stage from childhood to adulthood (*Kagitcibasi, 2002*).

This chapter is concerned with hypotheses as to how the adolescent, male and female, will adjust to the future when they are expected to be the leaders of tomorrow. In this twentyfirst century, there are paradoxical moves by the leading older generation comprising a heterogeneous group consisting mostly of politicians, businessmen and persons in the corporate world, setting the path of progress. This path is expected to be led by the present adolescent generation for the future population of the country. The path may be easy or difficult, dependent upon the adolescent's individual ability, coping mechanisms motivation and the need to achieve. We predict that it will be tremendously difficult as the future generation is facing crises in all spheres: political, economic and social, which they will have to contend with for which they should have the necessary potentials. However, as this twentyfirst century stands, it is one that has many ramifications that barrier the pathway of the young generation.

Generally speaking, the major barriers relate to education and job opportunities, especially among the poor section of society. This is because the current generation is living in a state of "confusion worst confounded" in the above cited areas. To put it succinctly, the majority of youngsters have not been educated to the extent that they should in order to be competent to obtain jobs that are suitable to their potentials. The utmost that they can achieve, especially in the rural areas, where they abound, is a high school education. Politically and socially, most adolescents belong to the category of the forgotten poor. They are ruled by the bureaucrats, who have better knowledge than they do about the world around them. In a sense, they live a life of ignorant bliss about themselves as participatory citizens in the conduct of national affairs.

Most human beings are born with an inherent identity. Usually, their first identity is as sons and daughters of the family into which they are born. Unfortunately, many of them do not know the social labels attached to the social categories in which they are born. If one were to enquire, in the rural areas, when was the child born, at the most they will give some such answer as near "some socio-religious event" of which they are familiar with. It is mainly those children who are born in hospitals who have registered names and, therefore, have a first identity of being the son or daughter of such and such person with a complete address. These days the government is rigorously pursuing citizens, especially of the lower categories who have no birth certificates, to have their names registered with complete information about themselves *(pehchaan patra)* so that they are aware of their identities as a citizen of India. This first identity is a legal name, placement in a family and, therefore, a family name. Later as the child grows into an adolescent, he comes to know of his or her other identities connected with the place of his birth, family, kin group, caste group, religious group, ethnic group, the geographical group, the State and the country. Most of all, he is very assured of his religious identity.

In this chapter, we are concerned with other aspects of his identity, mostly related to his knowledge and his information systems. For example, knowledge of the relationships that his caste has with other castes and his social, religious, and ethnic group.

The young adolescent needs to have his own perception of who he is and how the perceptions of others place him in the sphere of his family and community. If he is of a low caste, he generally tends to have a low self-esteem of his identity because his caste is considered to be lowly by the members of other castes which are placed on a higher level than his caste in the social hierarchy of the Indian caste system. If he belongs to a high caste group like the Brahmin, he perceives to be high in self-esteem. India being a caste-divided patriarchal society, being a person belonging to a Scheduled Caste, Scheduled Tribe, or a disadvantaged minority community like Muslim and also being a member of the female gender can give him or her a perception of low status in society (*Dube, L., 1988*).

Therefore, we are dwelling on the various categories to which an adolescent belongs at one and the same time. Homogeneously he is an Indian, but he has also an identity at micro level as he belongs to one of the many heterogeneous groups.

When we consider the perception of the adolescent about himself, we are talking about his psyche; his inner perception of himself and his perception of how others perceive him, especially others in his peer group. This cross perception is extremely important for a sense of identity or *belongingness* as to who he is. Another depth of perception is his psychological characteristics, namely his sense of dependency or independency his self-control, his understanding of his place in his family, his society and his ethnic group which gives him or does not give him a sense of stability (*Ainsworth, 1967*).

The other type of perception is his sense of belief in his own strength to attain a status which indicates his self-control in his perception of his identity. He is propelled along a pathway for obtaining an opportunity to identify himself.

He has also to understand the world of modernity *vis-à-vis* the world of traditionality. If we examine the demographic parameters of India, it is evident that the majority of adolescents, forming about 25 per cent of the total population, do not belong to the developing rungs of the country like the townships, the cities and the metropolitan areas. The adolescents in the metropolitan areas and cities and townships represent proportionately a miniscule number in contrast with the widespread number of adolescents living in rural and tribal areas and in *mofussil* (small district) township. Therefore, when we try to place the Indian adolescent, it is necessary to remember that he comes from different traditionally-oriented caste, ethnic, regional and such affiliative group backgrounds. Identifying himself in any one of these categories, either gives him his strength of mind and the power to contend or not contend with the barriers which confront him along his pathway towards adulthood. The average Indian adolescent from these diverse affiliative backgrounds has been socialized for the most part in a world of traditionality. New ideas, innovations, and technologies pose challenges to him as to whether he can contend with them successfully or not. Such challenges place him in a situation where he is compelled to ponder over the meaning of being of a person of a particular religion, of a particular ethnic group, of a particular region and, therefore, the strength of his self-identity and self-esteem is based on these attributes/traits. New ideas and technologies may instil in an individual, whose adolescent years were firmly rooted in traditionality, a sense of dynamic stability or instability, where he has to contend with new and upcoming modern technologies and lifestyles.

The recent socio-political and economic phenomena of globalization and liberalisation have confronted the adolescent with many challenges to the Indian adolescents. In the increasing interaction with the rest of the world is globalization. Within this whirlpool of modernisation, the Indian adolescent attempts to imitate the ways of the western world, the process of which is termed modernisation. These two concepts of globalization and modernisation interact dynamically.

Globalization has originated from the western world when they have reached to the eastern world on the knowledge that the eastern world is becoming better profiled in terms of market economies and the opportunities they offer for transaction. China gives the most evidence of this process. It is called the crouching tiger as it is lurching forward to rival the developed Western economies. The Middle East being a large storehouse of energy and since energy is widely sought by the western world, this area of the world is another one to focus on by the western world. India is attempting to rival China in making strides in the development of the global market economy and technology. There have been many exchanges between India, America and the European countries in commercial enterprises in interaction to create a network of commerce, industry and in the production of heavy equipment where each benefits from the other.

Wealth and status are attained mainly by professional skills, innovative genius and the knowledge of and proficiency in modern technologies. But, the vast majority of Indian adolescents growing up into adulthood have no easy access to these sources of knowledge and information and to building up of their cognitive and innovative capacities, so as to build up their cognitive and technical skills.

The truth of the matter is that the Indian youth has a long way to go in overcoming many barriers. In India, the joint family ethos still encourages large family sizes. Census data indicates a growing life expectancy which then means a larger number of elderly persons dependent upon the productive capacity of the current adolescents. The adolescent may not currently perceive these problems as they advance upon him, but in the large sphere and context of a mixture of globalization which the country has now embarked upon, these challenges are bound to descend upon the growing adolescent. Therefore, India will have many tongs in the fire for the young to contend with. The first question is, who is modernized? Certainly not the 70 per cent rural population who are only learning to imitate what little they see of the urbanite. It is only a small number of urbanite adolescents who are currently attending schools, learning technology, attempting to gain professionalism, who are becoming competent to take care of the young and the elderly in their families and society and even so, the country does not have adequate infrastructures and trained personnel to cope with the complexities growing by leaps and bounds in their habitat. There are large number of adolescents in the majority of poorer section who are not as well-educated, not as well-informed, nor have the achievement-motivation to increase their knowledge and information base. It is already said that, leave alone the divide between the north and the south of the world, it is the increasing divide within the country which will cause further destabilization within the dynamics of traditionality and modernity. The country under the present worldwide recession is contending with high consumerism and a rising cost of living. In this situation, the large majority of adolescents face the ability and frustration to be able to reach anywhere close to where the rich elite youngsters have reached.

Therefore, there are mixed combinations in the search for identity for the adolescent. For, the adolescent comes from many heterogeneous categories with which he has to live, such as belonging to a caste, yet also belonging to a socio-economic class, and yet again coming from a certain geoecological area. These are the problems that he has to face within his environment in order to arrive at a stability between himself and the demands of the world around him.

If we move into the micro ecological circle, there are many internal contentions. The parents will continue to have less effect on the value systems of their adolescents since the adolescents are attached to their peer groups and might have different aspirations in contrast to their parental generation. For, as they grow in the socio-psychological dimensions, they are more attuned to their peer group norms than parental norms. Further, the more they are attuned to the Western world, the greater is their need for making their own decisions about their own lifestyles, being responsible for their outcomes and creating a hiatus between their aspirations and those of the older generation.

All this while, we may have been assuming that the adolescent male and female is accultured to the same societal norms, the same ecology and the same socio-religious values. This is far from the fact. Having known that there are 26 States and 9 Union Territories, several official languages, several ethnic groups and sub-cultures in several ecologies, one can understand the magnitude of differences in each one of these sub-strata as contrasted among others. What is available to one sub-culture may not be available to another. One example is the variegated information sought or given in newspapers of marriage advertisement. Further problems which will beset the youth of today who will be the adult of tomorrow are the loosening of the joint family network and the increasing dependency upon the nuclear family structure. There is also the growing need for having double incomes in the face of the rising consumer pricing system.

As to be expected, there is much contention between the values of the youth and the elderly. The older group conform to traditional socio-religious beliefs, while the youngsters attempt to become modernised. The latter want to set up their own independence in their own way. If we view the behaviour of youngsters in the top echelons of the urban segment, they are fast growing into ways and customs that would even astonish the Western world. Such behaviour as pub-drinking, living together as partners without marriage, exchanging partners, moving from one broken marriage to another, are some oddities of behaviour confronting the adolescents (*Appadurai, B., 1997*). Yet, if one turns the mirror towards the rural and tribal geoecologies of the majority, who are really Indian in the totality of their make-up, these differences in duality of roles are staggering.

There is yet time to assist the poor adolescents raise their status, by extending reservation, by giving subsidies for education and scholarships for those who show marked tendencies towards competence. If these aspects are neglected, it stands to reason that only a few will continue to be at the top and will continue to rule the roost, while the rest will struggle to maintain a poor status of life. Who can hold the reins? It is nothing sort of a reorientation of the Governance system where more poor children are brought into the arena of reinforcement of their abilities and opportunities and being involved in the participation of their own programmes. They will be committed to the progress of their own betterment. The adolescent at this point of time is between confusion and conformity or as Erickson puts it is in an identity situation. The adolescent lives in a curious world where he is an *anomie* (*Erickson, 1950*) and where he does not or has not been reinforced by his networks, both family and social, to find his identity and become an enterprising self-actualising young adult (*Maslow, A.H., 1954*). The adolescent is growing in an environment where there is no known parameters of cohesion of values. Given the fact that India is a pluralistic, caste-divided, ethnically stratified culture, this attempt to find a collation of supportive value systems becomes a difficult search.

The upper class and caste adolescents have better opportunities to a system of education that encourages broadening of horizons and knowledge through the technology of new events in the current world system. This acquisition enables them more self-confident, to reason logically and to account for their actions. Unfortunately, with the lower class, not only is there poor infrastructure, untrained teachers, but also an apathy on the part of the parents to monitor the education of their adolescents (*Majeed, A., and E.S. Ghosh, 1982*).

Saraswathi's description of adolescent in different settings offers great insight into the psychological and unconscious workings of the inner mind (*Saraswathi, T.S.*). A high quality of parenting evoke more emotional stability in an adolescent (*Albuquerque, Z.M.; J.K. Rao; S. Rao; D.K. Subbakrishna; and G.G. Prabhu, 1990*).

Coping mechanisms are a central aspect of psychological adjustments of the adolescent (*Kashyap, L., 1996*).

Therefore, the three nexuses that influence adolescent identity are the parents, peers, and the world of social media and change which operate subtly to influence the internal workings of the adolescent's identity. The adolescent's psyche becomes fragile when he has to contend with his sexual needs *vis-à-vis* conformity with the social ethos in his community. At the same time, he is attracted to more information and innovative ways of living set by the world of liberalisation and modernisation. In the struggle between the three nexuses, he has to emerge as a well-knit unit, much like the way a chrysalis grows into a butterfly.

Moving towards coping mechanisms, the female is encouraged to behave in a feminine way as an adolescent, while the male is encouraged to build up his masculine virility. These differences in physical growth and psychological mannerisms serve the purpose of perception differentiation, both from the point of view of self-perception and other's perception of the self.

There is a strong relationship between the formation of identity and the dimensions of family attributes, namely cohesion, adaptability and communication. In this case, it is usually the parental figures, especially the nurturants, which affect the characteristics of the growing adolescents. In some families, the mother might have a greater influence, in others the father, and yet in some others, the grandparents. Further, the adolescent may be more attached to one family member rather than another. Therefore, there are various types of attachments among members of a family which influence adolescents in determining their unity and entity as growing individuals. High levels of family cohesion and adaptability tend to reinforce the healthy development of identity among adolescents. This identity is strengthened further by open communication of adolescents with their parents (*Bhushan, R., 1993*).

As the child develops from the pre-school through the primary school years, the child's physical and mental functionality is expected to increase. This is influenced by the various experiences he meets with, which are accumulated, during these phases of pre-school/primary school years. Every step, literally and figuratively, is geared towards the goal of gaining self-control and self-confidence. This is essentially at the time when the child is learning to wean away from the adult's attempts to retain him under parental control.

Biologically, the child has an inherent ability to use his own mechanisms of mind and body directions to select his own pathway. This is observable in early childhood when the child begins to indicate his resistance in having his own way. Negativity is one of the indices of his refusing to follow the parental pathway. As he grows older, he is influenced by peers during the primary school years and more especially during the adolescent years. As an entity, he selects those mechanisms which he admires and which he wishes to imitate from the behaviour of peers and elders surrounding him. When he looks backward through his earlier years, he realises that they are individuals whom he reveres and whose behaviour he imitates through social learning.

Besides this self-directed movement, he realises that his behaviour is unique to himself and the behaviour he wishes to imitate is added to his own unique repertoire. Childhood bondage and dependence in the early years are strands from which he wishes to detach himself and become a unique personality in himself. Therefore, his growing maturity helps him to seek his own identity *(Erickson, H.,* 1963). However, the lifestyle of an individual is one of continuity and discontinuity as he grows from one phase to another *(Ruth Benedict, 1938; Saraswati, T.S., and R. Dutta, 1988; Mead, M., 1958; Eleanor E. Maccoby, Theodore M. Newcomb and Eugene L. Hartley)* . Much of it has to do with cultural mores. He also experiences changes in psychological thinking such as the development of anxiety, of guilt, and shame, as the negative aspects and, on the other hand, he begins to develop a muscular niche, and gains self-esteem and self-achievement in an expansive way. A female, on the other hand, becomes less tom boyish, develops physical features of a growing woman and mental aspects of being coy, reticent, shy and in some respect, seductive. These two separate pathways of growth in maturity of behaviour of the males and females indicate the beginnings of heterosexuality and the attraction for the other sex, covert or overt [*Elias, J. and Elias, V.D. (1975)].*

The assumption in the description of identity attainment is not without its characteristic inconsistencies. Researchers have found that ego involvement is the predominant fulcrum in the maintenance of identity. The major findings indicate: identity achievement, moratorium, foreclosure and identity diffusion [*Marcia, J.E (1966)*]. The most stable attribute has been found to be identity achievement, where there is little crisis in terms of stability. Here, the adolescent can accept/reject a point of view so long as he has control over his "path direction". Hitches occur in the next phase of development into youthhood, namely moratorium on behaviour which is not to his liking, foreclosure on behaviour that is not acceptable to his peer groups and the moderation of identity diffusion. An adolescent's identity that has attained the status of moratorium (calling a halt to a current status) is related to the directions, the goals of the parents or elders, to which the adolescent agrees with some misgivings or compromise. Foreclosure, of the ego, implies willingness to agree to parental directions and goals set for him by the parents, in spite of some reluctance. Identity diffusion of an ego implies erraticism. Here the ego is willing to change and already decided upon an objective. If better opportunities do appear, the ego has no misgivings about change in goal-direction and, therefore, change within himself. He is either to go along in any direction that is worthwhile from his egoistical perception. These differentiations indicate that, inconsistencies in the ego are likely to occur in an unpredictable manner.

However, the adolescent in India has also to contend with the development of his identity in a given framework. The framework is made up of his culture, geoecology, and economic and political spheres. More especially, however, the adolescent is exposed to ***betwixt and between*** traditionality and modernity. His pathway is succoured and supported by his family members if they are in agreement with him. In many traditional families this is not so, and often there is a confrontation between elders in the family and the adolescents. This usually happens when the adolescent wishes to move along one pathway while the elders insist he should follow another.

Adolescent identity, therefore, is composed of generic as well as individual attributes. All human beings have a general identity of belonging to the human race. At the same time, the individual develops his own specific chromosomes and structural development which set him aside as a unique entity [*Malhotra, S., 2003*]. As the child grows in a family, whether joint or nuclear, he develops a psyche, which within itself is a complex internal fight as he meets with the complexity of the experiences surrounding him. For example, in a group of peers, he may be not sure who his real friends are, or who is helpful in times of need. Or which among his peers will come forward to help him, when he is caught in a complex web. Some adolescents require adult support in making decisions and yet others can do so on their own, for they have learned to disengage themselves from the support that adults wish to give. For example, he may find himself confused as to which girl friend of his is really loyal towards him.

An adolescent in India knows that he is an Indian, but from this generic make up, he has many dual semi-personalities, for he may be an Indian from north, south, east or west and yet at the same time, he may be as dedicated to a particular frame of religious fervour unlike others and yet like some others. The implication here is that adolescence is a generic term, usually pertaining to an age range and yet at the same time denoting that the identity of several adolescents is unlike each other.

Take for instance, a reputed college. Adolescents in that college could be attuned to a singular college philosophy and yet come from different families of orientation and still yet maintaining a personality dissimilar from others. These variations are likely to cause more confusion when the adolescent is new to a college or a high school where he has to find his own identity among several strangers who also have their own identity.

An individual may not be wholly attuned to only one category of individuals, but he might change this categorical frame from time to time dependent upon the situation he or she faces, and either discards it or assimilates it. This, therefore, implies that an adolescent has several frames of reference and if successful in life he can adjust to each frame adequately. For example, a new college entrant into a college in the North East, while he himself may be from south India, meets with great challenges to reconcile the differing cultural characteristics. In fact the ability to adapt to each one of these different frames is a mark of success in building up one's personality and finding one's identity with which he or she is most comfortable.

Living in a family the individual or the 'I' is perceived differently by parents, by grandparents, by siblings and by other relatives. Similarly, he is differentially perceived by friends and more closely by his nearest friends. The ability of the adolescent to move easily from one frame of identity to another as indicated by clues in his environment often makes a successful understanding of one's identity as perceived by others. These varying perceptions surrounding the adolescent are operative at the one and same time and yet require of the adolescent an ability to amalgamate all these into one holistic perception of him. This perception has necessarily to coincide with the perception of others of him so as to bring about equilibrium in these variegating perceptions. When there is dissonance among these perceptions it creates a sense of instability about his identity as perceived by others. For example, a group usually tends to have one individual as the leader and the other as followers. The leader has to be able to identify the personalities of those around him in order to get along with them, and often times even in this group, there are isolates who are personalities unable to adjust to the group because of the lack of understanding of the variations and the personalities of the group members as perceived by him (*Moreno, J., and H.H. Jennings. 1947*).

If the individual has an overall perception of his identity linkages, he is more in control and less confused. However, the journey that most adolescents go through is not smooth sailing. There are many ups and downs. For example, an oversized male may feel ashamed about his size in the presence of others who are less weighty than him. Females from *dalit* caste might find something is lacking in them in relation to the upper caste females. A male adolescent from Tamil Nadu may find that his peers are smirking about his spoken English language since his sentences sometimes have a twist in them. For example, he might say, "Twinkle twinkle little starow, yow I wonder what you yarrow, yupp yupp, boww boww, above this skyaa, so highya highya." and so on. And a Bengali adolescent might say, "I don't have a bheena, can you sing Bhocal?", where it is evident that the "V" is pronounced as "Bh". Thus, not only are the Indian adolescent variegated by their characteristic demographic details of caste, class, religion, ethnicity, but also by smaller differences like language pronunciation, gestures of the hand and even attitudes to certain aspects of life. Yet, the miracle of these is that all these adolescents come together to study in one college, where one frame of reference is offered to them. True, they might form their own gang. But the fact remains that they are all adolescents of Indian origin. One of the most striking differentiations that is marked is the philosophical aura to which they subscribe. Most Indian adolescents being brought up in close-knit families where traditionality is high. They find themselves in modernizing institutions and, therefore, are caught between the traditional modes of behaviour learned at home and the modernizing behaviour to which they are exposed in out of home situations. They, therefore, require the skill, the ability, and the perception to know how to behave in different fora. This is observable in the CEO community. They behave in highly modernized manner in five-star hotels and yet, at home, they are caste abiding, removing their slippers before entering the *puja* room and touching the feet of elders. Many of them may proclaim that they are vegetarian. But it is not unusual to observe that these vegetarian-eating individuals are quite at home with non-vegetarian food in restaurants. The ability to balance traditional behaviours and modernizing behaviour at one and the same time with flexibility and a perception that these can be intertwined at any time and disengaged at any other time is often the hallmark of the modernising adolescent and consequently the modernizing adult.

Identity is, therefore, an amalgam of behaviour traits which are exhibited in the company of others as to where possible the person originates from, which part of the country and the kind of behaviour which differentiates him from others.

It is possible to include these differentiated semi-identities into a seeming "oneness". The behaviour of one human being with another can be gauged by symbolic gestures, by facial expression and by positive and negative vibes they generate. It is the generalized others who perceive the adolescent as being apart from the rest that makes for unity in identity. Defining identities give a sense of shared identities. If one does not accept these variations in the formation of an identity, then the perception is confused and distorted. This generation of identity begins from early years and gets moulded and remoulded by experiences that are accrued from day-to-day to makeup a wholesome individual which is uniquely different from others. It is during the period of adolescence that his characteristic traits present a holistic picture of an individualized adolescent, male or female.

Most Indians as they go through an education system are also exposed to several facets of other Indians. In the holistic character of the Indian, for example, Hindi music is appreciated by me or the 'I' identity, at the same time 'I' appreciate South Indian dances or English poetry, or learning about a tribal culture, although the "I" belong to any one of these three. These various traits are absorbed into the identity called 'I'. There are 4635 communities in India with which "I" can identify with (*K.S. Singh's 2000, Mega Projects*).

Identities of the adolescent are socially constructed. This construction develops over the primary school into the adolescent years where the particular adolescent has certain identifiable characteristics, indicating to which group he belongs (caste, class, religion and region). It is when the perception of others and the perception of the adolescent are in tandem that one can say the given adolescent has an identity which is "similarly" perceived by him and others around him.

The adolescent has to introspect as to who he is, whom he belongs to and his place in each one of these groups with which he intermixes.

Therefore, the period of adolescence is highly significant for the development of an identity without confusion and one that is in tandem with variations in traits of other personalities with whom he interacts and yet retain his own unique identity.

REFERENCES

Ainsworth, 1967, *Infancy in Uganda: Infant Care and the Growth of Love.* Baltimore: John Hopkins University Press.

Albuquerque, Z.M.; J.K. Rao; S. Rao; D.K. Subbakrishna; and G.G. Prabhu, 1990, Stress and Coping in Psychologically Distressed and Non-Distressed College Students, *Indian Journal of Psychological Medicine*, 13, 63-70.

Appadurai, B., 1997, *Modernity at Large: Cultural Dimensions of Globalisation*. New Delhi: OUP.

Bhushan, R., (1993), "A study of adolescent identity achievement as related to family functioning variables", *Psychological Studies*, 38(1), 1-6.

Dube, L., (1988). 'On the Construction of Gender: Hindu Girls in

Patrilineal India', in K. Chanana (ed.), *Socialisation, Education and Women: Explorations in Gender Identity*, pp. 166–92. New Delhi: Orient Longman.

Elias, J. and Elias, V.D. (1975), The Sexual World of the Adolescent. *Counselling Psychology*, 5(1), 92-97.

Erickson, (1950), *Childhood and Society*. New York: Norton.

Erickson, H., (1963), *The Beginnings of Identity, in Childhood and Society*. p. 211. Hogarth Press.

K.S. Singh's (2000), Mega Projects), *ibid*. 115.

Kagitcibasi, (2002), *Rites of Passage to Adulthood: Adolescence in the Western World, Human Development*, 45 (2), 136-40.

Kashyap, L., (1996), *Measurement Issues in Family* Centred Social Work. In S. Bharat (Ed.), Family Measurement in India, New Delhi: Sage Publications.

Majeed, A., and E.S. Ghosh, (1982), A Study of Social Identity in Three Ethnic Groups in India, *International Journal of Psychology*, 17 (4), pp. 445-463

Malhotra, S., (2003), "Sŏcio-Cultural Diversity and Ethnocentrism in Child Mental Health", in G.J. Young, P. Ferrari, S. Malhotra, S. Tyano, E. Caffo (eds.), *Brain, Culture and Development*, Delhi: Macmillan India Ltd.

Marcia, J.E (1966), Development and Validation of Ego-Identity Status. *Journal of Personality and Social Psychology*, 3, 551-558.

Maslow, A.H., (1954), *Motivation and Personality*. New York: Harper and Brothers.

Moreno, J., and H.H. Jennings. 1947. 'Sociometric Control Studies of Grouping and Regrouping', Sociometry Monographs, 7.

Ruth Benedict, (1938), Continuities and Discontinuities in Cultural Conditioning. *Psychiatry, 1:161-167; Saraswati, T.S., and R. Dutta, 1988, Invisible Boundaries: Growing for Adult Roles. New Delhi: Northern Book Centre; Mead, M., 1958, "Adolescence in Primitive and Modern Society", in Eleanor E. Maccoby, Theodore M. Newcomb and Eugene L. Hartley (eds), Readings in Social Psychology*. pp. 341-49. New York: Henry Holt and Co.].

Saraswathi, T.S., (1999), Adult-Child Continuity in India: Is Adolescence a Myth or an Emerging Reality?", in T.S. Saraswathi (ed.), *Culture, Socialisation and Human Development*, 213-232. New Delhi: Sage Publications.

Index

CONCEPT

7/0/14/9/15

AJAY